Additional Praise f
Despair to Faith

"*From Despair to Faith* heralds a welcome development in the scholarship exploring the depths of Kierkegaard's relationship to the Christian spiritual tradition. Historically and theologically sensitive, Barnett's study of Kierkegaard's 'icons of faith' subtly serves as an important corrective to the many incomplete but persistent stereotypes of this challenging Christian thinker and equally shows him to be a spiritual author on the order of such enduring guides as John of the Cross and Johann Arndt."

Joel D. S. Rasmussen
University of Oxford

"This book may change not only your way of reading Kierkegaard but even how you shelve your books. That is to say, if you have been parking your Kierkegaard collection right after the nineteenth-century German Idealists or else intermingled with the twentieth-century existentialists, Barnett's argument will incline you instead to set Kierkegaard's religious discourses, at least, up on that special shelf you reserve for books that get to the heart of the Christian life, alongside similar writings by Augustine, Luther, and Bonhoeffer."

Andrew J. Burgess, Professor of Philosophy Emeritus
University of New Mexico

"Christopher Barnett's scholarship is operating at the forefront of a deepening appreciation of Kierkegaard's thought. In a beautiful assimilation of word and image, Kierkegaard's contribution to devotional literature shines through in Barnett's profound and fluent exposition. Barnett's book is essential reading for scholars and students, and, perhaps above all, to those interested in the heights, depths, and pathways of spirituality."

Simon D. Podmore
Liverpool Hope University

"In this sophisticated and sensitive reading, Christopher Barnett resists the common temptations to polemicize or fragment the thought of Søren Kierkegaard. Rather, he carefully demonstrates that there is a unifying focus in Kierkegaard's thought, namely, the conviction that the spiritual life is a homecoming, a return to God. To this end, Barnett illuminates how Kierkegaard persistently displays the intense human desire for that which brings fulfillment in concert with the Christian claim that the triune God can best satisfy that desire. In doing so, Barnett provides a much-needed theological reading of Kierkegaard that firmly places him in the fecund tradition of Christian spirituality and iconography."

Paul Martens
Baylor University

From Despair to Faith

From Despair to Faith

The Spirituality of Søren Kierkegaard

Christopher B. Barnett

Fortress Press
Minneapolis

FROM DESPAIR TO FAITH
The Spirituality of Søren Kierkegaard

Cover image: Copenhagen Harbour by Moonlight/Johan Christian Dahl/WikiArt
Cover design: Laurie Ingram

Library of Congress Cataloging-in-Publication Data
Print ISBN: 978-1-4514-7469-5
eBook ISBN: 978-1-4514-8747-3

The paper used in this publication meets the minimum requirements of American National Standard for Information Sciences — Permanence of Paper for Printed Library Materials, ANSI Z329.48-1984.

Manufactured in the U.S.A.

This book was produced using PressBooks.com, and PDF rendering was done by PrinceXML.

For my wife, Stacy, with gratitude.

Amore,

acceso di virtù, sempre altro accese.

–Dante

Contents

Abbreviations for Kierkegaard's Works

Danish[1]

SKS	*Søren Kierkegaards Skrifter* (1997–2013)
Pap.	*Søren Kierkegaards Papirer* (1909–48)

English[2]

CUP1	*Concluding Unscientific Postscript to "Philosophical Fragments,"* Vol. 1 (1992)
EO1	*Either/Or*, Vol. 1 (1987)
EO2	*Either/Or*, Vol. 2 (1987)
EUD	*Eighteen Upbuilding Discourses* (1990)
FT	*Fear and Trembling* (1983)
JP	*Søren Kierkegaard's Journals and Papers*, Vols. 1–7 (1967–78)
KJN	*Kierkegaard's Journals and Notebooks* (2007–)
LD	*Letters and Documents* (1978)
M	*"The Moment" and Late Writings* (1998)
PC	*Practice in Christianity* (1991)
PV	*The Point of View* (1998)
SLW	*Stages on Life's Way* (1988)
SUD	*The Sickness unto Death* (1980)
TD	*Three Discourses on Imagined Occasions* (1993)
UDVS	*Upbuilding Discourses in Various Spirits* (1993)
WA	*Without Authority* (1997)
WL	*Works of Love* (1995)

---

1. See the Works Cited section for complete details.
2. With the exception of *Søren Kierkegaard's Journals and Papers* and *Kierkegaard's Journals and Notebooks*, all abbreviations in this list correspond to editions of *Kierkegaard's Writings*, edited by Howard and Edna Hong. Again, see Works Cited for more information.

Preface

Literary critic Harold Bloom has defined "genius" as "a mystery of the capacious consciousness."[1] What he means by this phrase is not as puzzling as it may seem. For Bloom, the genius has the peculiar ability to imagine and to engender an abundance of perspectives, both of and beyond the time period in which she lives. This, however, is not an isolated capacity. Through the creative process, the genius also deepens and expands the awareness of her audience. For that reason, a work of genius affects persons in ways that a merely clever one cannot. Genius, quite literally, shapes the persons who encounter it, even if this impression will not be as broad as the consciousness that produced it.

Bloom himself classifies Søren Kierkegaard's genius as an openness to the "power of wisdom,"[2] but, in such an opinion, he is hardly alone. As George Pattison puts it, "[T]he list of philosophers, theologians, writers and artists who owe an acknowledged debt to [Kierkegaard] reads like a *Who's Who* of Western culture over the last hundred years."[3] Indeed, if anyone can be said to have had a

1. Harold Bloom, *Genius: A Mosaic of One Hundred Exemplary Creative Minds* (New York: Warner Books, 2002), 5.
2. Ibid., xiii. Also see 189ff.
3. George Pattison, *Kierkegaard and the Crisis of Faith* (London: SPCK, 1997), 1.

"capacious consciousness," surely it is Kierkegaard. But this strength has—as Bloom predicates of all geniuses—served to complicate the historical reception of Kierkegaard. Commentators have analyzed, characterized, and categorized him in innumerable fashion. Furthermore, certain aspects of his authorship have risen to the fore, often due to the particular interests of interpreters, rather than to his own broader emphases. Hence, for better or for worse, a brief pseudonymous work such as *Fear and Trembling* has garnered far more attention than the lengthy, signed *Upbuilding Discourses in Various Spirits*. Incomplete views of Kierkegaard have resulted, and a number of these perceptions have hardened into stereotypes. "The melancholy Dane," "the father of existentialism," "the unhappy lover": these and other notions, despite their limitations, have come to color the reception of Kierkegaard. On the other hand, important features of his life and thought have been marginalized, if not utterly forgotten. Such may be the cost of genius, but it need not be a *fait accompli*.

The aim of this work is to shed light on an aspect of Kierkegaard's authorship that has received insufficient attention—namely, his spirituality. That is not to suggest, of course, that Kierkegaard's religious thinking has been ignored altogether. It has been well documented that Kierkegaard wrote a great deal about Christianity, not from the disinterested perspective of an outsider, but as one who shared (or endeavored to share) the Christian faith. And though Kierkegaard is still viewed primarily as a philosopher, it is also true that many studies have examined, say, his understanding of Christ or his accent on Christian love. At the same time, however, Kierkegaard's standing as a spiritual author remains underdeveloped. By "spiritual author" this book means one who writes with an eye to "the preparation for, the consciousness of, and the effect of . . . a direct and transformative presence of God."[4] Put more simply, a spiritual author does not merely reflect on the grammar and logic of a given faith but, rather, seeks to involve the reader in that faith.[5] As will be seen, these and other related themes play a decisive role in Kierkegaard's authorship, thereby situating him among Christian spiritual masters such as John of the Cross and Johann Arndt. It is time, then, to investigate his spirituality more fully, to elucidate it for those who are keen to know more about Kierkegaard's understanding of the self's journey to God.

This book will be divided into five chapters. Chapter One will survey Kierkegaard's Pietist upbringing and his interest in Catholic and Protestant spiritual literature, as well as clarify his own category of "upbuilding." Chapter Two will introduce Kierkegaard's understanding of the interior life, paying particular attention to what he sees as each human being's decisive spiritual itinerary: the passage from despair to faith. Chapter Three will serve as a bridge of sorts. It will point out that, despite his warnings about the dangers of "the aesthetic," Kierkegaard was fond of illustrating faith by what he terms "pictures" of godliness. Can this apparent contradiction be reconciled? This chapter will argue "yes," reasoning that, for Kierkegaard, aesthetic imagery can serve in the manner of icons, rather than idols.

In turn, the final two chapters will explore Kierkegaard's images of godliness or, as I prefer, "icons of faith." Chapter Four will explore how Kierkegaard uses pictures of the natural world—from birds and flowers to the ocean—to represent faith in God. Chapter Five will

4. Bernard McGinn, introduction to *The Essential Writings of Christian Mysticism*, ed. Bernard McGinn (New York: Modern Library, 2006), xiv.
5. Gregory S. Clapper has argued that Kierkegaard's contribution to Christian spirituality lies in his understanding of "how theology and spirituality should be related to each other" ("Relations Between Spirituality and Theology: Kierkegaard's Model," *Studies in Formative Spirituality 9* [1988]: 161). However, he limits himself to this formal consideration, rather than investigate the ways in which Kierkegaard attempts to foster "the personal assimilation of [Christian] truth" (Ibid.). The goal of this text, in contrast, is to demonstrate that Kierkegaard does more than provide a theoretical framework for the importance of spirituality; he seeks to make it real.

extend this topic to the human realm, demonstrating how Kierkegaard depicts certain biblical figures as "icons of faith." For him, in other words, persons such as John the Baptist, the Apostle Paul, and the woman who was a sinner embody faith in a variety of ways. Thus they serve as exemplars for persons who long to grow closer to God.

Those who are familiar with my research to date—above all, my previous book, *Kierkegaard, Pietism and Holiness* (Ashgate, 2011)—will recognize that this work is an extension or, better yet, an application of the historical-cum-textual work preceding it. To understand Kierkegaard's personal involvement in the rich, multifaceted movement of Pietism is to understand that his own oeuvre is, in a number of respects, a reworking of Pietist themes—themes that themselves hark back to the wider tradition of Christian spirituality. In other words, given the importance of spirituality in Kierkegaard's own life and reading, it only makes sense that some kind of spirituality would be present in his writings.

And yet, I am aware that the issue is not so straightforward. There is, of course, the obligation of scholarly accuracy and integrity, which is the lot of everyone in academe. But there is also the fact that this text commits *me* to an interpretation of Kierkegaard that its predecessor did not. That is to say, whereas *Kierkegaard, Pietism and Holiness* largely (if not exclusively) concerns a historical reconstruction of Kierkegaard's relation to the Pietist movement, this book aims to establish a particular way of reading Kierkegaard. Thus it is an idiosyncratic effort. It does not feign to present "the whole Kierkegaard," nor does it claim to offer the only way of understanding the Dane's work. And while its findings may very well have implications for the philosophical and theological questions churned up by Kierkegaard, it will not be confused with a treatise on Kierkegaard as a philosopher of religion or as a systematic theologian.

That is not to suggest that such matters are irrelevant, only that they are not dealt with comprehensively here. In a sense, then, my task is at once ambitious and simple: I want to treat Kierkegaard's oeuvre as a place where one's relationship with God can be illuminated and deepened, and, in doing so, I hope to provide fresh insights into Kierkegaard's writings, especially those dealing with spiritual awakening and upbuilding.

Ideally, this book would find a broad audience—scholars and students, to be sure, but also non-specialist readers. Thus I have made its critical apparatus as straightforward as possible (perhaps a quixotic aim in Kierkegaard research!) and have tried not to overburden it with footnotes. Quotations from Kierkegaard's published work generally have been taken from the current standard English translations of his work, *Kierkegaard's Writings*, issued by Princeton University Press under the direction of Howard and Edna Hong. On occasion, however, I have elected to provide my own translations of Kierkegaard's writings, and, when appropriate, I have made a note of that decision. Accordingly, the standard Danish edition of Kierkegaard's works, *Søren Kierkegaards Skrifter* [SKS] is also indicated.[6]

Quotations from Kierkegaard's *Nachlaß* have been taken from two places: either *Søren Kierkegaard's Journals and Papers* [JP], the seven-volume set arranged by the Hongs, or the new (and still in progress) *Kierkegaard's Journals and Notebooks* [KJN], which is under the general editorship of Bruce H. Kirmmse. As with the published writings, I have cross-referenced the journals and papers to SKS as well,[7] though, in rare instances, I have needed to use the older

6. Full citations list the text in question, the volume number (when apt) and the page number(s): for example, SKS 7, 41 / CUP1, 34.
7. Volume number, journal designation, and journal entry number are provided for SKS, while volume number and entry number are supplied from the Hong edition: for example, SKS 17, AA:13 / JP 3, 3245. When KJN are used, only the volume number is added, so as to avoid

Papirer.[8] In addition, a register of abbreviations has been included, and complete documentary information can be accessed in the Works Cited section.

———————

Finally, before moving on to the book itself, a few words of acknowledgement are in order. This book was started while I was teaching at Berry College in Rome, Georgia, and I would like to sincerely thank all who helped me while I was there, especially the members of the Department of Religion and Philosophy and, above all, the Dean of the Evans School of Humanities, Arts and Social Sciences, Tom Kennedy. I have since moved on to Villanova University, where I have been welcomed by more people than I can begin to enumerate. However, I would be remiss if I failed to mention my department chair, Peter Spitaler, as well as my faculty mentor, Marty Laird, both of whom have encouraged my research in a number of ways. Needless to say, I have also benefited from the attention and insight of many persons working in Kierkegaard scholarship. Once more, it is impossible to list everyone, so I would like to mention those who have furthered this particular project in one way or another: Andy Burgess, Abraham Khan, Vincent McCarthy, George Pattison, Simon Podmore, Peter Šajda, Brian Söderquist, Jon Stewart, and Sylvia Walsh (with added thanks to Clark Elliston, to whom I first pitched the idea for this book over breakfast at the St. Giles' Café in Oxford). Lastly, I would like to

redundancy with the SKS (after which the KJN is modeled): for example, SKS 17 / KJN 1, AA:10.

8. These citations will be formatted as follows: *Pap.* V B 227 / JP 2, 2114.

thank Michael Gibson and everyone at Fortress Press for their interest and support.

This book is dedicated to my wife, Stacy, who had no idea where all this would lead but married me anyway.

Christopher B. Barnett
Bala Cynwyd, Pennsylvania
May 2014

1

Kierkegaard as Spiritual Writer

Books about Kierkegaard frequently open with a survey of his life. A number of reasons might account for this development, not least the fact that Kierkegaard's biography contains drama worthy of Shakespeare. There are family secrets, unhappy love affairs, and public scandals, just to mention a few elements of his story. Moreover, Kierkegaard himself writes pointedly of these events, pouring over them in his journals and papers, but also alluding to them in his published writings. In this way, he not only leaves a great deal of material for his biographers, but also helps determine how they arrange and interpret his story.

To be sure, it is no accident that most versions of Kierkegaard's life focus on four issues: his complicated relationship with his father, Michael Pedersen Kierkegaard (1756–1838); his love for—and breakup with—his fiancée, Regine Olsen; his public dispute with *The Corsair*, a satirical Copenhagen paper; and his infamous "attack" on Denmark's state church. These are what might be termed the "crescendos" of Kierkegaard's life, and he himself certainly calls attention to them. And yet, even as musical crescendos are but conspicuous points within a larger and more varied composition, so are the crescendos of Kierkegaard's life prominent outgrowths of a larger and more subtle story. That is not to deny, of course, the importance of these biographical highpoints. Rather, it is to recall that they belong to a broader context, which deserves to be studied in its own right.

Such is the case with Kierkegaard's spiritual background. As will be seen, Kierkegaard came from a pious home, where devotion to God was encouraged as much as sin was discouraged, and this rearing influenced him throughout his life. As he puts it in an 1848 journal entry: "What I know [of Christianity] is not to my credit but is actually due to my father's upbringing."[9] M. P. Kierkegaard had a background in and an affinity for the spirituality associated with Pietism, and this connection—in addition to its impact on his youngest son—will be considered below. Strangely, however, biographies of Kierkegaard tend to neglect this aspect of his story. For example, the Pietist movement receives limited attention in Alastair Hannay's *Kierkegaard: A Biography*, so much so that "Pietism" is not even listed in the index.[10] Nor does the term figure into Joakim Garff's *Søren Kierkegaard: A Biography*.[11] To be fair, both works do mention the Moravian Congregation of Brothers, a Pietist group with which the Kierkegaard family was affiliated. But Garff only devotes two paragraphs to the subject[12]—a small number for a book that runs more than eight hundred pages—and Hannay's treatment is similarly brief.[13] Shorter "sketches" of Kierkegaard's life are not much different. In his recent *Kierkegaard: An Introduction*, C. Stephen Evans touches on Kierkegaard's familiarity with "evangelical pietism,"[14] but

9. SKS 21, NB 6:89 / JP 6, 6243.
10. Alastair Hannay, *Kierkegaard: A Biography* (Cambridge: Cambridge University Press, 2001).
11. Joakim Garff, *Søren Kierkegaard: A Biography*, trans. Bruce H. Kirmmse (Princeton, NJ: Princeton University Press, 2005).
12. Ibid., 11.
13. Hannay, *Kierkegaard*, 37.
14. C. Stephen Evans, *Kierkegaard: An Introduction* (Cambridge: Cambridge University Press, 2010), 5.

embeds this reference in a larger discussion about M. P. Kierkegaard's personal failings. The topic does not turn up again.

One could speculate about why Kierkegaard's Pietist background seems to be of marginal interest to biographers, but such a discussion exceeds the scope and interest of this work. What *is* needed, however, is an exploration of Kierkegaard's links to the Christian spiritual tradition. This will not be an exhaustive discussion,[15] but, at its conclusion, Kierkegaard's emergence as a spiritual writer in his own right should no longer seem accidental.

Kierkegaard's Spiritual Background

As alluded to above, Kierkegaard's particular spiritual vision grew out of contact with Pietist—and, by association, Catholic[16]—sources. "Pietism" can be defined as a devotional movement that developed within Lutheranism toward the end of the sixteenth century and spread to other Protestant denominations throughout the seventeenth and eighteenth centuries. Given its breadth, it is unsuitable to talk of Pietism as if it were a unified development. However, in all of its manifestations, Pietism sought to promote holiness—the fulfillment of Christian life and activity—in the church as well as in the world. This purpose was thought urgent on account of the various troubles

---

15. However, as noted in the Preface, I have dealt with this issue in depth elsewhere. See, for example, Christopher B. Barnett, *Kierkegaard, Pietism and Holiness* (Farnham: Ashgate, 2011).

16. At the same time, Kierkegaard's connection to Catholicism cannot be *reduced* to the influence of Pietism. On the contrary, Kierkegaard had a multifaceted interest in Catholic authors and ideas, from Augustine's stress on resting in God (as will be discussed in Chapter Two) to the spiritual insights of Alphonsus de Liguori. On the latter point, see Cornelio Fabro, "Influssi Cattolici Sulla Spiritualità Kierkegaardiana," *Humanitas* 17 (1962): 501-07. For broader considerations of Kierkegaard's connection to Catholicism, see Jack Mulder, Jr., *Kierkegaard and the Catholic Tradition: Conflict and Dialogue* (Bloomington, IN: Indiana University Press, 2010), as well as my "Catholicism," in *Kierkegaard's Concepts: Absolute to Church*, ed. Steven M. Emmanuel, William McDonald and Jon Stewart (Farnham: Ashgate Publishing, 2013).

afflicting post-Reformation Europe, from theological division to political strife to plague.

Wherever they were found, Pietists were recognized for their emphasis on devout habits and practices. Among other things, they wrote hymns, founded schools, formed charitable organizations, coordinated Bible studies and prayer groups, sought ecumenical dialogue, encouraged moral renewal, and popularized numerous edificatory writings. John Wesley (1703–1791)—the founder of Methodism, an English incarnation of the Pietist movement—once recounted a "common way of living" among Methodist missionaries:

> From four in the morning till five each of us used private prayer. From five to seven we read the Bible together. At seven we breakfasted. At eight was the public service. From nine to twelve I learned German, Mr. Delamotte, Greek; my brother wrote sermons, and Mr. Ingham instructed the children. At twelve we met together. About one we dined. The time from dinner to four we spent in reading. . . . At four were the Evening Prayers, when either the Second Lesson was explained (as it always was in the morning), or the children were catechized and instructed before the congregation. From five to six we again used private prayer.[17]

Such piety attracted praise, but more than a little disparagement also followed. One critic snickered that the name of Wesley's group "was first given to a few persons who were so uncommonly *methodical* as to keep a diary of the most trivial actions of their lives, as how many slices of bread and butter they ate . . ."[18] Similarly, the general label "Pietism" first achieved currency in the 1680s, serving largely as a term of abuse until the German Pietist, Philipp Jakob Spener

---

17. John Wesley, "A Short History of the People Called Methodists," in *The Works of John Wesley*, ed. Rupert E. Davies (Nashville: Abingdon, 1989), 9:428.
18. Quoted in John Wesley, "A Second Letter to the Rev. Dr. Free," in *The Works of John Wesley*, 9:324.

(1635–1705), embraced it as denoting one "who studies God's Word/ And also leads a holy life according to it."[19]

Though its practical emphases could (and did) slip into mere social activism, Pietism originated first and foremost as a spiritual movement—that is to say, as a movement of *inner* renewal, which took its direction from some of Catholicism's great mystics.[20] This,

---

19. Quoted in Carter Lindberg, introduction to *The Pietist Theologians*, ed. Carter Lindberg (Oxford: Wiley-Blackwell, 2005), 3.

20. Here, and elsewhere in this text, words such as "mystic" and "mystical" are used in general fashion, indicating, for example, persons who seek to relate to divine mystery or treatises that strive to facilitate such a relationship. Understood in these terms, the difference between a spiritual work and a mystical one is negligible. Still, it must be said that the mystical has often been associated with unusual and privileged experiences of the divine, despite the fact that a number of so-called "mystics" have questioned the nature of such experiences or, at least, the ability of human words to articulate them. For that reason, I prefer the broader and more contemporary language of "spirituality," though, at times, I draw on the vocabulary of mysticism, particularly where it is historically appropriate to do so. This usage, however, should neither be confused with a systematic appraisal of the questions surrounding "mysticism," nor with an assumption that such questions have been settled. For a précis of this complicated issue, see Alister McGrath, *Christian Spirituality: An Introduction* (Oxford: Blackwell, 1999), 5-7.

Incidentally, the extent to which Kierkegaard might be considered a "mystic" (in the strong, experiential sense mentioned above) is an interesting problem. In a well-known journal entry—dated May 19, 1838 and timed precisely as 10.30 a.m.—Kierkegaard writes of "an indescribable joy," "a heavenly refrain," that "glows all through" the believer (SKS 17, DD:113 / JP 5, 5324). Some commentators have associated this passage with a proper mystical experience (see, for example, Jean Wahl, "Kierkegaard et le Mysticisme," *Hermès* 1 [1930]: 16-23), while Joakim Garff has wondered if the whole thing was made up, a poetic musing and nothing more (Garff, *Kierkegaard: A Biography*, 128). Lending credence to the latter standpoint is the fact that Kierkegaard, writing as Assessor Wilhelm in *Either/Or*, is actually critical of "mysticism" (SKS 3, 237 / EO2, 248). On the other hand, as this study will make clear, and as I (and others) have noted elsewhere, Kierkegaard had a great affinity for spiritual literature, much of which could be deemed "mystical" on some level. What can be deduced from this incongruity? Putting off to the side the status of Kierkegaard's *own* religious experiences, which obviously remain unknowable to others, it seems safe to say that he *cautiously* appropriates mystical concepts and themes. That is to say, though he does not place great emphasis on mystical experience per se—and, via the Assessor, indicates the trouble with the single-minded pursuit of such experiences—he borrows notions such as "detachment" from mystical writers and incorporates them into his spirituality, which, at any rate, is not meant to appeal to isolated hermits but, rather, to those seeking faith amid the ambiguity of modern life. As Peter Šajda writes, "[T]he medieval mystics are part of a broader paradigm of practical Christian spirituality, which served Kierkegaard as a counterpoint to contemporary Christendom, which rid itself of essential emphases common in older traditions" ("Kierkegaard's Encounter with Rhineland-Flemish Mystics: A Case Study," in *Kierkegaard Studies Yearbook 2009: Kierkegaard's Concept of Irony*, ed. Niels Jørgen Cappelørn, Hermann Deuser, and K. Brian Söderquist [Berlin: de Gruyter, 2009], 584). This is the sort of spirituality that will be investigated in what follows.

indeed, was the main intention of the so-called "father of Pietism," Johann Arndt (1555–1621). A Lutheran pastor, Arndt concluded that the greatest problem facing the still new Protestant impulse was a disregard for the individual's vocation to holiness. Persons *are* saved by faith, he acknowledged, but faith is supposed to issue in a converted heart and in a consecrated life. Claiming the former in the absence of the latter is, to borrow a phrase used by Dietrich Bonhoeffer centuries later, a cheapening of grace.

In order to get this message across, Arndt boldly began to publish the writings of Catholic mystics—particularly those of Johannes Tauler (1300–1361) and Thomas à Kempis (ca. 1380–1471). He also composed his own spiritual treatise, *True Christianity*, which explicitly drew on the mystical tradition. Unsurprisingly, this approach garnered a great deal of criticism from certain Protestant quarters. However, Arndt maintained that these Catholic authors offered insights crucial to the full flowering of faith. Why? First and foremost, Arndt lauded their Christ-centered spirituality. For him, they did not understand faith as a mere cognitive assent to Christian teaching but, rather, stressed that true faith also sees Christ as the "example, mirror and rule for life."[21] Second, and following on from the previous point, Arndt called attention to the mystics' identification of Christlikeness with a detachment from, or a denial of, inordinate worldly pleasures and things. This emphasis led to a third point, also endorsed by Arndt: the person of faith neither can nor should try to achieve a likeness to Christ through self-will or through self-mastery. On the contrary, faith's most basic detachment is from the person's false belief in his own power. When, through faith, one comes to see that one is "nothing,"[22] the internal activity of God will bring one to holiness and, with it, to Christlikeness.

---

21. Johann Arndt, *True Christianity*, trans. Peter C. Erb (New York: Paulist, 1979), 39.
22. Ibid., 208.

These mystical principles—which by no means can be limited to Tauler and Thomas à Kempis, but, in one form or another, traverse Catholic spirituality—were bequeathed by Arndt to his Pietist heirs. That, in fact, is how Kierkegaard came into contact with them. M. P. Kierkegaard grew up on Denmark's windswept Jutland peninsula—a rustic area, which had seen an influx of Pietist clergy and groups during the first half of the eighteenth century. There, far from the increasingly secular capital city of Copenhagen, M. P. Kierkegaard was schooled in Pietist spirituality, with its emphases on self-denial and the imitation of Christ. As a youth, financial circumstances forced him to leave home in search of a better life in Copenhagen. He took up with his uncle and, through a combination of hard work and good fortune, eventually became one of the wealthiest businessmen in Copenhagen. Yet, he never separated from his Pietist connections and, as a result, his humble beginnings.

During the latter years of the eighteenth century and the first few decades of the nineteenth, Pietism emerged as a bastion for an "authentic" form of Christianity, which held fast to traditional Christian doctrines over against the rationalistic modifications of the Enlightenment. In Copenhagen, a small but vocal collection of state church priests embraced the Pietist cause. However, it was the local Moravian society that most prominently advanced this effort. M. P. Kierkegaard, for his part, immersed himself in both of these Pietist channels, attending churches with Pietist-minded clergy, while also participating in the Moravian community. Not only did he frequent its Sunday evening worship services, but he even served on the society's governing board. These close ties were maintained until his death. Copenhagen's Moravian leader, Johann Matthiesen, later remembered him as a "faithful brother in the true sense of the word," who approached the society's affairs "with particular love."[23]

Not surprisingly, M. P. Kierkegaard's children were also a part of the Moravian community. They attended the Moravian meetings with their father, and they were introduced to Pietist ideas and literature. To be sure, a number of Søren Kierkegaard's habits and interests can be traced back to his relationship with Pietism. In a narrow sense, for example, there is Kierkegaard's fondness for many of the classic writings of the Pietist tradition—a tradition that, as mentioned, stretches back to medieval Catholicism. A survey of Kierkegaard's library holdings reveals this affinity. Works by Tauler, Thomas à Kempis, Arndt, and even Wesley appear. But those are just the more prominent names. Numerous other authors with connections to Pietism also turn up, from Catholics such as Henry Suso and François Fénelon to Protestants such as Gerhard Tersteegen and Hans Adolph Brorson. This wide selection of spiritual literature is one of the distinguishing aspects of Kierkegaard's library.

Equally noteworthy, however, are Kierkegaard's frequent references and allusions to these writings, particularly in his journals and papers. Time and again he invokes the above writers as spiritual masters, whose insight and wisdom are steady guides amid the tumult of life. They belong, he notes, to an "older"[24] time, when the true exigencies of Christian existence—namely, constant growth in the spiritual life, with an eye to Christ as one's pattern—prevailed over the self-serving interests of careerist churchmen and professional thinkers. For him, to turn to the Pietist literary tradition is to be encouraged and strengthened, rather than dispirited and enervated. Kierkegaard's preferred word for this process is "upbuilt." Thus he writes in 1848, "I am currently reading [Tauler] for upbuilding

---

23. Quoted in Kaj Baagø, *Vækkelse og Kirkeliv i København og Omegn* (Copenhagen: Gads Forlag, 1960), 21. All translations from foreign-language titles are mine, unless otherwise indicated.
24. See, for instance, SKS 8, 206 / UDVS, 102 and SKS 23, NB 18:39 / JP 4, 4926.

[*Opbyggelse*],"[25] and he refers to Arndt's *True Christianity* as an "upbuilding writing [*Opbyggelsesskrift*]."[26]

Indeed, the second, broader influence that Pietism had on Kierkegaard was the concept of "upbuilding" itself. It is a notion whose spiritual implications go back to the Bible, as when Paul tells the Corinthians that his apostolic mission is "for building up and not for tearing down" (2 Cor. 13:10).[27] This sort of usage, of course, is borrowed from the word's literal sense, which has to do with the practice of putting something together for the sake of a desired end. As a building is "built up" from a variety of pieces into a cohesive structure, so, Paul implies, can a person (or group) be "built up" from a state of fragmentation to one of unity. Thus the term not only bears connotations of improvement, but also of completion, fulfillment.

As has been seen, Kierkegaard recognized that the upshot of the Pietist literary tradition was spiritual upbuilding. Yet, from an early age, he also would have encountered the idea of "upbuilding" at Copenhagen's Moravian society. The society attributed its significant popularity during the first few decades of the nineteenth century to the city's need for, and the Moravians' provision of, spiritual edification. As Johannes Christian Reuss—Copenhagen's Moravian leader from 1815 to 1835—once put it, "[T]he greatest number come Sunday after Sunday, so there is surely no doubting that they seek and find upbuilding [*opbyggelse*], which one then also hears many remarks about."[28] The lone extant fragment of Reuss's Sunday evening talks reveals that, for him, spiritual upbuilding results from a humble openness to Christ's mercy and grace. Sin may impede the person's growth in holiness, but it does not have the last word. As Reuss explains, "Our Savior takes pity on us, he knows our hearts, knows

---

25. SKS 20, NB 4:102 / JP 2, 1844, my translation.
26. SKS 8, 206 / UDVS, 102. Also see SKS 23, NB 18:39 / JP 4, 4926.
27. All biblical quotations are taken from the NRSV.
28. Quoted in Baagø, *Vækkelse og Kirkeliv*, 23.

our sinfulness, knows how we need help, comfort, strength and encouragement in order to live for him and proclaim his death by living in humility, love and according to his mind and heart."[29] Other aspects of the community's life—from its liturgical celebrations to its circulation of Arndt's *True Christianity*—only reinforced this emphasis.

That Kierkegaard, then, would later devote a notable portion of his authorship to "upbuilding discourses" can hardly be taken as an accident. The Pietist influence here is unmistakable. But how, exactly, did he understand the concept? This question will be dealt with below, not only for its own sake, but also in preparation for a larger consideration of Kierkegaard's spirituality—a consideration that constitutes that principal business of this book.

The Upbuilding in Kierkegaard

On May 16, 1843, Kierkegaard published a short collection entitled *Two Upbuilding Discourses*. It came on the heels of his breakthrough work, *Either/Or*, which had shaken Copenhagen literary circles just three months earlier. The difference between these two efforts is pronounced. Issued pseudonymously, *Either/Or* is a sprawling juxtaposition of an aesthetic worldview—punctuated by musings on suicide, boredom, and seduction—and an ethical one that eulogizes middle-class satisfaction and civic industriousness. In contrast, *Two Upbuilding Discourses* bears Kierkegaard's own name, and it contains a pair of quiet reflections on passages from the Bible. Taken by itself, this literary concurrence might be written off as a fluke. Yet, on October 16, 1843, Kierkegaard published three new works—the pseudonymous treatises, *Fear and Trembling* and *Repetition*, as well as

29. Quoted in ibid., 23–24.

the signed *Three Upbuilding Discourses*. Thus a pattern emerged, and it would come to characterize Kierkegaard's authorship.

Indeed, over the course of his career, Kierkegaard issued a number of signed upbuilding writings, frequently in conjunction with pseudonymous philosophical works. Kierkegaard himself describes this arrangement as an instantiation of his theory of communication. As with all communicators, his efforts begin with a particular goal in mind—in his case, to make people aware of the religious and, more specifically, of the Christian.[30] What is unique is that he does not presume that persons are ready to encounter this objective. Thus two sorts of writings are needed. The first type adopts nonreligious points of view. For Kierkegaard, this is a matter of meeting people halfway, so to speak, since most persons either misunderstand or distort the nature of the religious. Thus religious truth becomes clear only after the limitations of other worldviews (Kierkegaard tends to describe these standpoints as either "aesthetic" or "ethical") have been explored from the inside out. This is the aim of the pseudonymous writings. In contrast, the signed upbuilding writings are "directly religious."[31] They communicate a religious message openly and, in turn, ensure that his ultimate goal is present at every stage of his authorship.

More than a little ink has been spilled over this authorial strategy. Yet, as far as this work is concerned, the relevant point has to do with Kierkegaard's equation of the upbuilding and the religious. For him, one is built up toward the religious, even as the religious is upbuilding. The two go hand in hand.

But this point is not as straightforward as it may seem. For one thing, Kierkegaard is clear that the sheer fact that something is religious—or has religious significance—does not mean that it is upbuilding. An 1849 journal entry, for instance, distinguishes

30. SKS 13, 19 / PV, 12.
31. SKS 13, 14 / PV, 7–8.

between a system of Christian doctrine and the upbuilding. The former seeks "to comprehend faith" and, for that reason, can dangerously treat faith as a mere intellectual exercise.[32] The latter, on the other hand, concerns the development of an individual human life. As Sylvia Walsh explains, "Claiming the upbuilding as 'his' category as a poetic writer, Kierkegaard cast his…upbuilding discourses…to 'that single individual', which every human being 'is, can be, yes, should be' before God."[33] Thus the upbuilding is not an academic subject or a scholarly pastime but, rather, a means toward human fulfillment, valid both in "calm weather" and "when it storms."[34] It neither beguiles nor diverts, but *strengthens*.

Similarly, Kierkegaard also makes clear that the upbuilding should not be conflated with authoritative Christian communication. That is not to say, of course, that such communication necessarily fails to edify. But the upbuilding, as Kierkegaard sees it, ranges beyond magisterial teaching and sermonic injunction.[35] This conclusion is partly grounded in Kierkegaard's analysis of the human self—an analysis that, as will be discussed in the next chapter, obtains for all human beings, regardless of their religious background. It is also grounded in Kierkegaard's own literary mission and status. Though he had formal academic training in theology, he was never ordained into priestly ministry. As a result, many of his upbuilding writings contain a disclaimer about his lack of ecclesiastical authority, as well as an admission of his personal need for edification. The strengthening of the upbuilding, then, cannot be reduced to a particular time or place, to a particular office or institution. It involves the religious life at its most basic level, with the self's inbuilt yet

---

32. SKS 22, NB 12:21 / JP 3, 3564.
33. Sylvia Walsh, "Kierkegaard's Theology," in *The Oxford Handbook of Kierkegaard*, ed. John Lippitt and George Pattison (Oxford: Oxford University Press, 2013), 294.
34. SKS 22, NB 12:21 / JP 3, 3564.
35. See, for example, SKS 7, 247-48 / CUP1, 256.

often frustrated desire for that which is everlasting and harmonious, as opposed to that which fades and tears apart.

This is one reason why Kierkegaard often writes of love in connection with upbuilding. Drawing on the words of Paul—who famously told the church in Corinth that "love builds up" (1 Cor. 8:1)—Kierkegaard asserts that the upbuilding "is exclusively characteristic of love."[36] Here he does not mean that all forms or manifestations of love are upbuilding. An erotic relationship can become twisted by greed and selfishness; a friendship can become warped by elitism and pride. Nor does Kierkegaard mean that love upbuilds at the *exclusion* of other activities. Indeed, he quotes Paul to the contrary: "[Love] does not insist on its own way" (1 Cor. 13:5).[37] What this statement means, for Kierkegaard, is that love has a noncompetitive relationship with the world. It does not have to get out of the way in order for another activity to take place. Rather, it is capable of "being able to give itself in everything, be present in everything."[38] In this sense, love is identical to upbuilding: "[E]verything can be upbuilding in the same sense as love can be everywhere present."[39] Kierkegaard illustrates this point with an example:

> We would not think that the sight of a person sleeping could be upbuilding. Yet if you see a baby sleeping on its mother's breast—and you see the mother's love, see that she has, so to speak, waited for and now makes use of the moment while the baby is sleeping really to rejoice in it because she hardly dares let the baby notice how inexpressibly she loves it—then this is an upbuilding sight. . . . Just to see the baby sleeping is a friendly, benevolent, soothing sight, but it is not upbuilding. If you still want to call it upbuilding, it is because you see love present, it is because you see God's love encompass the baby.[40]

36. SKS 9, 215 / WL, 212.
37. SKS 9, 215 / WL, 212.
38. SKS 9, 215 / WL, 212.
39. SKS 9, 216 / WL, 213.

Here Kierkegaard does not bother to account for the shift from "the mother's love" to "God's love." Elsewhere, however, he is clear that human love is but a sharing in the love of God, the "Eternal Love," who is the "source of all love in heaven and on earth," "so that the one who loves is what he is only by being in you."[41]

Hence, for Kierkegaard, there is an intrinsic bond between the upbuilding, love, and God. They comprise a type of trinity. Wherever love is present, so is the upbuilding. Yet, since God is love, it is also true that the presence of the upbuilding signifies the presence of God. Thus Kierkegaard's task as an upbuilding author is to manifest these connections, not in dogmatic fashion,[42] but in such a way that they come to develop the reader's spiritual life:

> To build up is to erect something from the ground up. In ordinary talk about a house, a building, everyone knows what is meant by the ground and the foundation. But what, in the spiritual sense, is the ground and foundation of the spiritual life that is to bear the building? It is love. Love is the source of everything and, in the spiritual sense, love is the deepest ground of the spiritual life. In every human being in whom there is love, the foundation, in the spiritual sense, is laid. And the building that, in the spiritual sense, is to be erected is again love, and it is love that builds up. Love builds up, and this means it builds up love.[43]

One might object that other facets of life are upbuilding—for instance, political competence, artistic skill, and scholarly erudition. But these talents, *sensu stricto*, do not concern themselves with love, and so Kierkegaard maintains that their upbuilding "is still not upbuilding in the deepest sense."[44] "This is because, spiritually, love is the *ground*, and to build up means to erect from *the ground up*."[45]

---

40. SKS 9, 217 / WL, 214.
41. SKS 9, 12 / WL, 4.
42. As Paul Müller puts it, "Kierkegaard proves himself a...*theologian*, — for the sake of upbuilding" ("Begrebet 'det Opbyggelige' hos Søren Kierkegaard," *Fønix* 7 (1983): 15.
43. SKS 9, 218 / WL, 215.
44. SKS 9, 219 / WL, 216.

To this point, then, it has been shown that Kierkegaard came out of a background (Pietism) that emphasized the importance of spiritual upbuilding. It also has been seen that he made this concern characteristic of his own authorship, especially in his composition of various upbuilding writings. These writings are broadly religious in both aim and content. More specifically, however, they involve the development of love in the reader—a love that, for Kierkegaard, originates from God and always registers the presence of the divine.

With these points established, Kierkegaard's status as a spiritual writer should already be coming into focus. The last section of this chapter, however, will attempt to make this link even clearer. It will do so by way of a general consideration of the nature of spiritual writing, in addition to a brief comparison of Kierkegaard's efforts with those of others in the genre.

Kierkegaard as Spiritual Writer

It has become a shibboleth to call the Western world "secular"—that is to say, preoccupied with the affairs and things of the present world, rather than with a sacred dimension within or beyond it. As is usual with such platitudes, this one contains an element of truth: the contemporary world has detached itself from the direct influence of religion, now treating science and technology—in a variety of manifestations, whether biological, physical, or social—as the determining factors in day-to-day life. But this development, despite its seeming ubiquity, has hardly erased religion from human consciousness. The declining influence of institutional religion is notable, but, on the other hand, there is a renewed, perhaps even unprecedented thirst for "spirituality."

45. SKS 9, 219 / WL, 216.

But what, exactly, is "spirituality"? The word itself is derived from the Latin term *spiritus*, rendered in English as "spirit." Although less than precise, this connection nevertheless indicates that "spirituality" concerns the immaterial aspect of human nature—that internal ground of the person, where the vicissitudes of life are contemplated and met. But this definition is still inadequate, for "spirituality" connotes more than a bare, computer-like processing of human experience. It also involves the quest to draw *meaning* from experience. Of course, the content of this meaning varies in accordance with an individual's background and inclinations. The spirituality of, say, a Muslim from Chicago differs from that of a Christian from rural Mexico. There is, however, a decisive similarity. In both cases—and in all examples of spirituality—the endeavor to locate meaning in experience looks beyond that which is simply historical or physical and instead seeks that which is ultimate. This is the *raison d'être* of spirituality. For its practitioner understands that only what is fundamentally and finally real can bring harmony out of the diverse and often contradictory notes of life.[46] To develop one's spiritual life is to journey, however slowly, from a state of disintegration and unrest to one of unity and calm.

This common purpose is one reason why "spirituality" is frequently seen as a field where interreligious dialogue is not only possible but fruitful. All human beings have a spiritual core and so are in search of ultimate meaning, whether consciously or

46. Kierkegaard himself alludes to this point, though he tends to speak in terms of "inwardness" [*Inderlighed*] rather than "spirituality" [*Aandelighed*]. The difference, however, is largely accidental, as "spirituality" had neither the currency nor the import that it does today. In an 1844 passage, Kierkegaard notes that "[i]nwardness is the eternal," which kindles in the person a "need" for God and, with it, the habit of prayer (*Pap.* V B 227 / JP 2, 2114). Elsewhere he adds that, when one neglects inwardness, "the spirit is finitized;" consequently, the cultivation of inwardness is a matter of "earnestness," whereby the person strives for that which is truly enduring (*Pap.* V B 65 / JP 2, 2112). These insights, which turn up throughout Kierkegaard's writings (albeit in varying guises), will be examined further in the next chapter.

unconsciously.[47] As has been mentioned, Kierkegaard's understanding and treatment of the upbuilding rests upon this presupposition. Many of his upbuilding writings operate on a humanistic level, focusing on the person's innate desire for love and, with it, happiness. Of course, in doing so, Kierkegaard does not exclude God as the spiritual life's origin and end. He assumes the biblical claim that God is love, and thus the task of building up love in the human being is, in the end, a movement toward the divine. But this objective is frequently more implicit than explicit in Kierkegaard's upbuilding writings, particularly in the ones dating from 1843–1844. For that reason, it is possible to view him as a spiritual writer in the broad sense indicated above. His spirituality not only *makes* a catholic appeal but *has* a catholic appeal, too.

At the same time, however, Kierkegaard was very much a *Christian* thinker, who penned a number of works that plainly involve Christian doctrines and themes. Signed efforts such as "What Meaning and What Joy There are in the Thought of Following Christ" and "It is the Spirit Who Gives Life," as well as pseudonymous writings such as *The Sickness unto Death* and *Practice in Christianity*, mark his later authorship. Already in these titles is adumbrated a more pronounced stress on the nature of God, on the problem of human sin, and, above all, on the imitation of Christ—subjects that disclose Kierkegaard's background in and development of Christian spirituality.

Just how these later spiritual writings relate to his earlier ones is a matter of debate. Do they represent a rupture in Kierkegaard's spiritual vision, so that it is more accurate to speak of Kierkegaard's

---

47. This claim is increasingly contested by materialist philosophy. Nevertheless, even Daniel Dennett—a so-called "Darwinian fundamentalist"—has acknowledged the universal benefits and relevance of spirituality. See Daniel Dennett, *Breaking the Spell: Religion as a Natural Phenomenon* (London: Penguin Books, 2007), 303.

"spiritualities" rather than his "spirituality"? Or do they ultimately serve to complement his prior works, functioning, so to speak, as two sides of the same coin? The present work assumes the latter view, which has been summed up nicely by George Pattison: "Although there is an undeniable shift in emphasis, vocabulary, style and thematisation between Kierkegaard's earliest and last religious writings . . . it is [not] possible to sustain an absolute distinction here."[48] As Pattison writes, and as has already been alluded to in this work, the question of the human condition in general, and of love in particular, erects an "interpretive bridge"[49] spanning Kierkegaard's various spiritual writings. To the extent that questions about existential meaning and destiny arise throughout Kierkegaard's corpus, points of overlap can be found between "the humanistic Kierkegaard" and "the Christian Kierkegaard." Theirs is a relationship of completion, not fragmentation.

Given the interests and scope of this work, it would be distracting, not to mention tedious, to expand on this point at length. Suffice it to say that it remains a "live" issue in the secondary literature,

---

48. George Pattison, *Kierkegaard's Upbuilding Discourses: Philosophy, Literature and Theology* (London: Routledge, 2002), 31. Thomas C. Anderson complements Pattison's position, though he is more interested in the Christian tendencies of Kierkegaard's humanistic discourses, rather than the humanistic tendencies of Kierkegaard's Christian output. See his "Is the Religion of *Eighteen Upbuilding Discourses* Religiousness A?," in *International Kierkegaard Commentary: Eighteen Upbuilding Discourses*, ed. Robert L. Perkins (Macon, GA: Mercer University Press, 2003), 51-75. A contrary position has been put forward by Anders Kingo, who views Kierkegaard's upbuilding discourses as essentially dogmatic in nature and therefore representing a break with the anthropological starting point typical of modern thinking. As he puts it, "Kierkegaard is a thinker of revelation [*åbenbaringstænker*]" (Anders Kingo, *Den Opbyggelige Tale: En systematisk-teologisk studie over Søren Kierkegaards opbyggelige forfatterskab* [Copenhagen: Gad, 1987], 25). Yet, this stance suggests a rift between nature and grace that, as will be seen below, is problematic for many spiritual authors, who perceive a degree of continuity between the natural and the supernatural. This study ought to provide support for the view that Kierkegaard falls into the latter camp, though it does not have pretensions of resolving the debate once and for all. After all, this issue extends well beyond the pale of Kierkegaard scholarship, becoming, arguably, the defining question of twentieth-century theology, which has involved thinkers as diverse as Karl Barth, Emil Brunner, Henri de Lubac, and Réginald Garrigou-Lagrange.

49. Pattison, *Kierkegaard's Upbuilding Discourses*, 193.

not least because of the various scholarly interests in Kierkegaard, some of which prize his humanism over his Christianity and vice versa. In this context, however, a more helpful approach would be to show that Kierkegaard's twin spiritual emphases—on an intrinsic human desire for that which brings fulfillment, as well as on the Christian claim that the triune God can best satisfy this desire—are hardly alien to the Christian spiritual tradition writ large. In other words, Kierkegaard's twofold approach to spirituality puts him in company with other great spiritual writers. This connection will be underscored by a survey of two spiritual authors with whom he had a degree of familiarity: Bernard of Clairvaux and Meister Eckhart. The claim here will not be that Kierkegaard's views are identical to these predecessors, nor that their approaches constitute a unified spiritual "school." At stake, rather, is a much more basic claim, namely, that their respective spiritualities highlight a common progression from human longing to divine fulfillment.

Bernard of Clairvaux

In his epistolary treatise, "On Loving God," the great Cistercian abbot Bernard of Clairvaux (1090–1153) begins by pointing out that human love—whether for God or for neighbor—is only possible because of the preceding love of the divine. His point here is quite literal. As Bernard sees it, human love cannot even get started without "food for everyone who eats, light for seeing, air to breathe."[50] Yet, he adds, these bodily needs are by no means the only gifts bestowed upon human beings, for persons also receive the three "higher goods" of dignity, knowledge, and virtue.[51] To consider the "natural man,"

---

50. Bernard of Clairvaux, "On Loving God," in *Bernard of Clairvaux: Selected Works*, trans. G.R. Evans (New York: Paulist, 1987), 175.
51. Ibid., 176.

then, is already to make out the presence of God. As Bernard explains, "There are two things you should know: first, what you are; second, that you are not what you are by your own power."[52]

Bernard later illustrates this point in more lucid fashion, paying particular attention to love. He notes that it is a "natural" passion, adding that "what is natural should be at the service of the Lord of nature."[53] But this service is not of one kind or quality. It has to develop gradually, beginning with an immanent, "this-worldly" focus. As Bernard writes, "[B]ecause nature has become rather frail and weak, man is driven by necessity to serve nature first. This results in bodily love, by which man loves himself for his own sake. He does not yet know anything but himself . . . "[54] According to this "innate" self-love, the person seeks to provide for his basic needs, including the necessity of getting along well with others.[55]

This process is not easy. It is inevitable that "tribulation" will arise, which leads to what Bernard calls love's "second degree"—the human being's turn to God "for his own sake, not God's."[56] This is the first gesture toward the eternal, whereby the person recognizes "what he can do by himself and what he can do only with God's help."[57] This stage of love, then, remains rooted in the desire for self-preservation.

And yet, the more a person calls upon God for help, the more she appreciates "how sweet the Lord is."[58] Thus there is an evolution into "the third degree of love, in which God is loved for his own sake."[59] But this is only the penultimate step of love. For, according to Bernard, even greater is the one who "loves himself only for God's

52. Ibid.
53. Ibid., 191.
54. Ibid., 192.
55. Ibid.
56. Ibid., 193.
57. Ibid.
58. Ibid., 194.
59. Ibid.

sake."[60] This is the point at which the human being unites with the divine. No longer curtailed by the "entanglements of the flesh,"[61] the person comes to will whatever God wills. One's self-concern is precisely concern for God. As Bernard puts it, "To lose yourself as though you did not exist and to have no sense of yourself, to be emptied out of yourself and almost annihilated, belongs to heavenly not to human love."[62] He likens this process to that of a drop of water that falls into a vat of wine and takes on its color and taste.[63] This, he adds, is the sort of love found in the "holy martyrs"[64] of the Christian faith.

Thus Bernard concludes with a definitive form of Christian *caritas*, albeit one that grows out of love's natural beginning. For him, in other words, that which is Christian does not break from the human but perfects it. The contours of human life unfold in the direction of Christian fulfillment. As will be seen, the spirituality of the great Dominican mystic Meister Eckhart (ca. 1260–ca. 1327) supports a similar, if not identical, point of view.

Meister Eckhart

Eckhart begins his short treatise "On the Noble Man" with an affirmation: there is an inherent "nobility" in the "created nature" of human beings, inasmuch as humans can be brought to a "divine" end through the grace of God.[65] The word "can" here is not incidental. For Eckhart, the person's growth toward his divine fulfillment is hardly a matter of course but, rather, must be won through a

60. Ibid., 195.
61. Ibid., 197.
62. Ibid., 195.
63. Ibid., 196.
64. Ibid., 197.
65. Meister Eckhart, "On the Noble Man," in *Meister Eckhart: Selected Writings*, trans. Oliver Davies (New York: Penguin Books, 1994), 99.

process—a gradual, and sometimes painful, cultivation of the "inner" or "noble" man.

Indeed, citing the Apostle Paul, Eckhart argues that human nature is not monolithic but complex. Juxtaposed with the divinely inclined inner man is the "outer man," who bears bodily concerns and temptations and thus serves as a channel through which evil can ensnare the inner man.[66] In this tension Eckhart sees a repetition of the fall of humanity, as depicted in the book of Genesis: the "inner man is Adam," the outer the "serpent."[67]

What, then, is the person to do? The good news, according to Eckhart, is that neither temptation nor sin can do away with the inner man: "[S]ince it is God himself who has engendered this seed, sowing and implanting it, it can never be destroyed or extinguished in itself, even if it is overgrown and hidden. It glows and gleams, shines and burns and always seeks God."[68] This natural impulse toward God, then, has to be developed. Eckhart, like Bernard, maintains that this is done through stages, beginning with what comes easiest and progressing to that which is most difficult. So one starts by imitating "the example of good and holy people," much as a child copies her parents.[69] But this concentration on external behavior has to be slowly left behind, evolving into a focus on the "teaching and counsel of God and divine wisdom" and, eventually, into an "eager devotion" to everything divine.[70] Such dedication will encounter opposition in the world. Hence, as one progresses, one must not only learn to endure trials and sufferings, but also to "live altogether at peace in [oneself], quietly resting in the overflowing wealth of the highest and unutterable wisdom."[71] Now one is ready for what Eckhart sees as the

66. Ibid., 100.
67. Ibid.
68. Ibid., 101.
69. Ibid., 101.
70. Ibid.

final stage of spiritual growth: "stripped" of all worldly cares, one is "drawn into and changed into an image of the divine."[72] The outer man has lost its power, and "eternal peace and blessedness reign."[73]

Hence, as with Bernard, Eckhart traces the correspondence between "the natural self" and "the religious self." In the gift of the former—a gift received by every human being—lies the seed of the latter. The spiritual life, then, is not extrinsic to human nature, imposed on a select number of persons by an alien and arbitrary power. Rather, it is already *there*, implicit in all human experience and merely awaiting active cultivation. The goal of the spiritual writer is to clarify this connection and, like a practiced navigator, to chart its course.

Conclusion

The examples of Bernard of Clairvaux and Meister Eckhart shed light on Kierkegaard's own status as a spiritual writer. Though his authorship may involve a variety of aspects and categories—the aesthetic and the religious, the genius and the apostle, the immanent and the transcendent—these features are in service to a larger purpose, namely, the flourishing of the human self. This flourishing is not static, but dynamic. It is not so much a birthright as a process. Moreover, for Kierkegaard, as for figures such as Bernard and Eckhart, that which is Christian does not foreclose on or interrupt this process but, rather, emerges out of it and marks its culmination.

The "progressive" nature of Kierkegaard's spirituality should become clearer over the remainder of this work. Later chapters will explore how Kierkegaard uses imagery to promote spiritual growth,

71. Ibid., 102.
72. Ibid.
73. Ibid.

so that faith is distinguished by an ever-deepening contemplation of certain "icons." First, however, it is necessary to summarize Kierkegaard's understanding of the interior life—an understanding that provides the anthropological and theological foundation of his spirituality. It is to that subject, then, that this study now turns.

2

Kierkegaard on God, Self, and the Spiritual Journey

While the goal of Chapter One was to establish Kierkegaard as a spiritual author, the purpose of this chapter is to examine the concepts that underlie his spiritual writings. Not surprisingly, this task must contend with the nature of God, but, just as importantly, it must involve the essence and structure of the human being. These emphases are hardly unique to Kierkegaard's authorship. Many of the Christian tradition's greatest theologians, including Augustine of Hippo and Thomas Aquinas, have recognized that the profession of God as creator has crucial ramifications for human nature. Likewise, the theme of a spiritual journey, so common among Christian mystics, presupposes that *someone* is searching, an "I" or a "you," a "him" or a "her." In other words, spirituality in general, and Christian spirituality in particular, must involve a conception of human nature. The spiritual writer has to know where human beings come from and who they are, if she is also to map out where they should be going and who they should be.

The aim of this chapter, then, is twofold. First, it will explore Kierkegaard's understanding of the human self—a topic that has been called "the unifying focus of all of Kierkegaard's writings."[1] In doing so, it will establish that Kierkegaard's anthropology is, at bottom, a theological anthropology, which situates the human self in ultimate relationship with the divine. Second, it will trace the various spiritual itineraries in Kierkegaard's authorship, culminating in *The Sickness unto Death*—one of Kierkegaard's masterpieces, which unpacks the self's journey from despair to faith. As will be seen, this path requires the slow but certain cooperation of the self, as it learns to detach from illusory affections and, eventually, to "rest" in her maker. This is faith, and in it consists human happiness.

God as the Origin of the Self

The theme of *exitus-reditus* or "exit and return" is a common one in Christian thinking. One can see it, for example, in the structure of Thomas Aquinas's *Summa Theologica*, which proceeds from the nature of God to the act of creation and on to the restoration of humanity to God through the moral and religious life. According to this model, God is both the origin and the end, the alpha and the omega (Rev. 1:8), of all being. In turn, God's creative activity is brought to the forefront, thereby showing that redemption—the journey back to God—satisfies the most basic impulse of the creature. As will be seen, this *exitus-reditus* model also characterizes

---

1. Arnold B. Come, *Kierkegaard as Humanist: Discovering My Self* (Montreal: McGill-Queen's University Press, 1995), xxi.

Kierkegaard's thought.[2] The process of "salvation" is only intelligible in light of creation; the spiritual life is a sort of homecoming.

With this in mind, it is not surprising that Kierkegaard's understanding of human nature actually begins with *theology*. God is the origin of the self, and, for that reason, the self cannot be understood without reference to God. This insight propelled the development of Kierkegaard's reasoning about God, which is exceptional neither for its systematic organization nor for its speculative majesty but, rather, for its concerted attempt to draw existential implications from classic Christian doctrines.[3] For Kierkegaard, theology sheds light on anthropology.

A significant, if oft overlooked, example of this tendency is found in Kierkegaard's treatise *The Changelessness of God*. Published in 1855, just a few months before his death, it is an exposition of one of Kierkegaard's most cherished biblical passages: "Every generous act of giving, with every perfect gift, is from above, coming down from the Father of lights, with whom there is no variation or shadow due to change" (James 1:17). Kierkegaard begins by noting that the text contains an implicit contrast between God, the "Father of lights," and the world. To observe the latter is to observe constant change: one moment gives way to the next; the sunrise comes and goes; each human being will one day die. "How depressing," notes Kierkegaard, "how exhausting, that all is corruptibility, that human beings are

2. That is not to suggest, however, that Kierkegaard's spirituality is fully convertible with the Neoplatonic tendencies associated with the *exitus-reditus* model—tendencies found in Christian thinkers such as Albert the Great, Thomas Aquinas, and Meister Eckhart, just to name a few. Nevertheless, the overarching theme of *exitus-reditus* is certainly present in Kierkegaard's thinking, and, as I have argued elsewhere, it bears the vestiges of his relation to Pietism and, in turn, to the medieval mystical tradition. See Christopher B. Barnett, "The Mystical Influence on Kierkegaard's Theological Anthropology," *Acta Kierkegaardiana* 6 (2013): 105–22. For more on the theme of *exitus-reditus* itself, see, for example, Alain de Libera, *Albert le Grand et la philosophie* (Paris: Vrin, 1990), 116–77.

3. Recently, this point has been fleshed out vis-à-vis Kierkegaard's understanding of the person of Christ. See David R. Law, *Kierkegaard's Kenotic Christology* (Oxford: Oxford University Press, 2013).

changefulness, you, my listener, and I!"[4] But there is good news. Above and beyond all of this change is God, whose good and perfect nature never varies. It is this truth that the Apostle James has disclosed, and, for Kierkegaard, it is "simply and solely sheer consolation, peace, joy, blessedness."[5]

The reason for this happiness has to do with God himself, who, as Kierkegaard explains, is changeless, omnipotent, omnipresent, pure, and luminous. He moves earthly affairs, but is not moved by them.[6] Here Kierkegaard effectively assumes what might be termed a "classical" understanding of God's nature. Whereas change involves unrealized potential, God is perfect and, therefore, fully actual. There is nothing unrealized in him, because he lacks nothing. To refer to God's immutability, then, is to bring out his absolute distinction from other beings. He alone is the creator.[7] Everything else is but a creature.

For Kierkegaard, these two general points—that God is radically other, and that God is the source of all being—correspond to one another. He makes this connection clear in an earlier journal entry, where he argues that human freedom is a sign of God's transcendent perfection. "The greatest good . . . that can be done for a being, greater than anything else that one can do for it, is to make it free."[8] And yet, he adds, only an omnipotent being can make another being free. A consideration of earthly power shows why this must be the case. First, if one with earthly power were to try to make another free, then that act, no matter how well intentioned, would put the other in one's debt. But a state of debt is hardly liberation. As Kierkegaard explains, "All finite power makes [a being] dependent

4. SKS 13, 328 / M, 269.
5. SKS 13, 330 / M, 271.
6. SKS 13, 330 / M, 271.
7. SKS 13, 330 / M, 271.
8. SKS 20, NB:69 / JP 2, 1251.

. . ."[9] Second, earthly power always carries with it a measure of "finite self-love."[10] It cannot give away without expecting *something* in return: the politician wants votes, while the artist craves applause. As Kierkegaard puts it, "[T]he one who has power is himself captive in having it . . ."[11] And if the giver is not free in giving, then the recipient is not free in receiving. At best, theirs is a relationship of *quid pro quo*.

It is not so with God, however. Deficient in nothing, and therefore requiring nothing from others, God is able to "withdraw"[12] even as he gives. God does not give at the expense of the recipient, nor does the recipient receive at the expense of God. Everything that one receives from God is part of the surplus of creation; there are no strings attached. For Kierkegaard, this power—namely, to give without encroaching on the recipient—specifies just why God is identified with goodness. "For goodness is to give oneself away completely, but in such a way that by omnipotently taking oneself back one makes the recipient independent."[13] But how is this possible? According to Kierkegaard, it is possible only because God is, as it were, on a different level of being than creatures. God does not compete with human beings, nor does he have need of their cooperation. "Omnipotence is not ensconced in a relationship to another, for there is no other to which it is comparable . . ."[14] In a nutshell, the relationship between God and humanity is *noncompetitive*. From God the human being receives the entire field of being and becoming as a gift. To go forth in the world as a free creature is precisely to realize that gift. Kierkegaard sums it up in

9. SKS 20, NB:69 / JP 2, 1251.
10. SKS 20, NB:69 / JP 2, 1251.
11. SKS 20, NB:69 / JP 2, 1251.
12. SKS 20, NB:69 / JP 2, 1251.
13. SKS 20, NB:69 / JP 2, 1251.
14. SKS 20, NB:69 / JP 2, 1251.

this way: "He to whom I owe absolutely everything, although he still absolutely controls everything, has in fact made me independent."[15]

Independence, however, should not be mistaken for self-sufficiency. For Kierkegaard, the self *is* free, but this freedom is properly employed when it leads the self to recognize its utter dependence on God—a recognition that, according to Kierkegaard, is often *"terrifying."*[16] This dread is the flipside of the joy mentioned above. For the self, in its freedom, can (and frequently does) fall prey to illusions. Not least among them is a poor conception of the divine. The self erroneously thinks of God in creaturely terms, assuming that God's will has changed or even that God has gone away, wearied by the sinful unfolding of world history.[17] In turn, a feeling of sheer autonomy or even isolation arises. No longer seen as a gift, the world now appears as so much merchandise, available for use and consumption.

Yet, as Kierkegaard concludes *The Changelessness of God*, he returns to where he started: God has not changed but, rather, is unchanged. God remains the eternal source of all being, including the human self. If this recognition initially results in "sheer fear and trembling"[18]—since God's transcendence seems to threaten the self's freedom—it will ultimately provide *"reassurance and blessedness."*[19] As Kierkegaard goes on:

> It is really so that when you, weary from all this human, all this temporal and earthly changefulness and alteration, weary of your own instability, could wish for a place where you could rest [*hvile*] your weary head, your weary thoughts, your weary mind, in order to rest, to have a good rest – ah, in God's changelessness there is rest [*Hvile*]![20]

15. SKS 20, NB:69 / JP 2, 1251.
16. SKS 13, 331 / M, 272.
17. SKS 13, 332–33 / M, 273–74
18. SKS 13, 336 / M, 278.
19. SKS 13, 336 / M, 278.

Here Kierkegaard echoes Augustine of Hippo's famous prayer to God: "[O]ur hearts find no peace until they rest in you."[21] Moreover, also like Augustine, he is keen to flesh out the unfolding "complexity of life,"[22] displaying how the dynamics of human existence disclose an innate religious sensibility and, finally, a genuine desire for union with God.[23]

Kierkegaard makes the changing self's relationship with the unchanging God central to his thought. As has been seen, he views God as the origin of the self. But this is only part of the picture. What remains to be discussed is his understanding of the nature of the self. Only then can the need for a spiritual journey, which culminates in faith, emerge with clarity.

20. SKS 13, 336–37 / M, 278. As will be seen throughout this work, the notion of "rest" plays a key role in Kierkegaard's spiritual thinking. Here he employs the word *Hvile*, which suggests a state of relaxation or an end to strained effort. This definition carries both psychological and physical connotations, as when a person is free from exhaustion or simply finished with the day's work. Elsewhere Kierkegaard uses the word *Ro*, which is quite similar, albeit with a stronger implication of "rest" or "calm" as a desired psycho-spiritual state, in the same way that one might seek *Ro* by a mountain stream or in a quiet chapel.

21. Saint Augustine, *Confessions*, trans. R. S. Pine-Coffin (London: Penguin Books, 1961), 21.

22. SKS 13, 337 / M, 279.

23. Though it is not a topic that has received a great deal of attention over the years, Kierkegaard's connection to Augustine is, indeed, significant. In his new book, Lee C. Barrett argues that both Augustine and Kierkegaard "presuppose that the human heart is restless and that its ultimate *telos* is God as the highest good;" moreover, he maintains that "Augustine and Kierkegaard make 'journey' the central metaphor for the Christian life" (Lee C. Barrett, *Eros and Self-Emptying: The Intersections of Augustine and Kierkegaard* [Grand Rapids, MI: Eerdmans, 2013], 22). In these tendencies, Barrett adds, Kierkegaard represents "an alternative to the dominant Lutheran nonteleological understanding of faith," since, like Augustine, he paradoxically aims to "encourage passionate human striving while simultaneously fostering a sense of absolute reliance on God" (Ibid., 22-23). As will be seen, these are themes that figure in my own analysis of Kierkegaard's writings. And though I have tended to link Kierkegaard's spirituality to Pietism and to certain strands of Catholic mysticism, Barrett is surely right that Augustine stands as an important influence on these (and other) traditions. As he puts it, "Augustine (or different theologically constructed Augustines) have served as the basic springboards for Catholic, Lutheran, Reformed, and even Wesleyan thought" (Ibid., 32).

The Nature of the Self

The stereotype of Kierkegaard is that he is an "individualist"—a thinker who presupposes the human being's primordial autonomy and, in turn, seeks to defend "the individual" from outside interference. However, the above discussion shows why Kierkegaard would not subscribe to such an individualism. After all, to the extent that he sees God as creator, he also sees the self as always already ensconced in relationships with God and with the entire sphere of creation. In turn, he does not equate "freedom" with the mere guarantee of autonomy; rather, it emerges when the self is in a proper relationship with others. Hence, in Kierkegaard, "even when we focus on the individual self, we find not a simple entity, but a complex relationship. As spiritual beings, humans are relational right down to the core, even on the 'inside,' so to speak."[24] So thoroughgoing is this view of selfhood that, in point of fact, Kierkegaard defines the human self as "the relationship" [Forholdet].[25]

But what, exactly, does this mean? Kierkegaard deals with this question in a number of his writings. The most famous instance is found in his 1849 treatise, The Sickness unto Death, which he published under the pseudonym Anti-Climacus. This text has been hailed as Kierkegaard's "most mature work, his masterpiece,"[26] and Kierkegaard himself said it was "extremely valuable."[27] Unsurprisingly, then, it is not a work that lends itself to easy summary, though its premise is perhaps simpler than its notoriously labyrinthine prose.

24. C. Stephen Evans, Søren Kierkegaard's Christian Psychology: Insight for Counseling and Pastoral Care (Vancouver: Regent College Publishing, 1990), 46.
25. SKS 11, 129 / SUD, 13.
26. Come, Kierkegaard as Humanist, xxi.
27. SKS 21, NB10:69 / JP 6, 6361.

According to Anti-Climacus, the human self has been fashioned as a combination of contrasting elements—namely, infinitude and finitude, temporality and eternality, and freedom and necessity.[28] Yet, these contrary components themselves are *not* the self; rather, the self is the third thing that emerges when this "synthesis" relates itself to itself. It is this free self-reflexivity that at once constitutes the human being's highest call and greatest danger. In the latter case, the self fails to harmonize its contraries, slipping, for example, into the wraithlike disengagement of infinitude or into the bourgeois worldliness of finitude. Anti-Climacus categorizes such states under the name "despair" [*Fortvivlelse*]. On the other hand, when the self brings its contraries into balance and tranquility, it roots out despair and is able to reach its full potential. Crucially, however, this realization can only happen when the self "in relating itself to itself relates to another."[29] This "other" is God, to whom the self owes its existence. In other words, the self's fulfillment finally depends on how it relates to its reason for being. As Anti-Climacus writes, "The formula that describes the state of the self when despair is completely rooted out is this: in relating itself to itself and in willing to be itself, the self rests transparently in the power that established it."[30]

The above formula compresses some of Kierkegaard's most central ideas into a few words. The notion of resting in God turns up, as has been seen, in *The Changelessness of God*. Likewise, Anti-Climacus's understanding of the self's internal structure and dynamism is anticipated in one of Kierkegaard's early upbuilding discourses, namely, 1844's "To Need God is the Human Being's Highest Perfection." In this short piece, Kierkegaard makes clear why the

28. SKS 11, 129 / SUD, 13.
29. SKS 11, 130 / SUD, 13–14.
30. SKS 11, 130 / SUD, 14.

self—conflicted and confused, yet capable of genuine peace and happiness—must undertake a spiritual journey.

As was his wont, Kierkegaard prefers to ease into his thesis in "To Need God." What is it, he begins, that a human being really needs? Proverbial wisdom, drawing on Scripture, says that it is the grace of God.[31] And yet, Kierkegaard continues, such wisdom often dulls people to the profundity of the matter. Clichés mingle with clichés, and soon people confuse God's grace with everything else in life: one should want it only in moderation.[32] From an earthly perspective, the person of great wisdom is distinguished by his indifference to material luxury and by his quest for self-sufficiency. However, for the one who is in a conscious relationship with God, the situation has been "inverted."[33] As Kierkegaard explains, "[T]he more he needs God, the more deeply he comprehends that he is in need of God, and then the more he in his need presses forward to God, the more perfect he is."[34]

But why is this the case? What is it about the human self that makes its dependence on God a necessity and, indeed, a perfection? The answer has to do with the self's inner dynamics. Though it is "the most glorious creation,"[35] the self is nevertheless caught in a struggle, "not with the world but with [itself]."[36] Here Kierkegaard is already working with material that will characterize *The Sickness unto Death*. As he goes on, the self is actually an interplay of two opposing selves—a "first self" and a "deeper self."[37] The former finds both sanctuary and pleasure in external phenomena such as material

---

31. Here Kierkegaard has in mind 2 Cor. 12:9, where Paul writes, "[The Lord] said to me, 'My grace is sufficient for you, for power is made perfect in weakness.' So, I will boast all the more gladly of my weaknesses, so that the power of Christ may dwell in me."
32. SKS 5, 294 / EUD, 300.
33. SKS 5, 296 / EUD, 303.
34. SKS 5, 296–97 / EUD, 303.
35. SKS 5, 301 / EUD, 308.
36. SKS 5, 301 / EUD, 308.
37. SKS 5, 306 / EUD, 314–15.

goods and earthly tasks. Yet, says Kierkegaard, these tangible things are unreliable and always already open to doubt. Thus the task of the deeper self is to call attention to the first self's erroneous confidence. It strives to convince the first self that it has entrusted its happiness to what "continually changes"[38] and so cannot be trusted at all.

This conflict between the outward and the inward results in a "painful situation."[39] The first self, despite its natural inclination, can no longer enjoy the external world and, in Kierkegaard's words, "is halted."[40] At this point, the first self is faced with a decision. It "either must proceed to kill the deeper self, to render it forgotten . . . or it must admit that the deeper self is right . . ."[41]

If the first self chooses the latter, the two selves are reconciled and genuine personal fulfillment becomes possible.[42] Indeed, the first self previously had assumed an ill-fated relation to reality: the external, changeable world sooner or later would have betrayed the first self's confidence. However, under the guidance of the deeper self, which forsakes dependence on externalities, one adopts a better relation to the world and thus obviates betrayal. Yes, there is a painful loss of immediacy, but gained is a truer understanding of the human being's place in the world and, with it, "the condition for coming to know [oneself]."[43] The victory of the deeper self, then, is not world-denying but, rather, world-affirming, insofar as the self is now able to construct its identity according to how things *are* rather than how they *seem*. As Kierkegaard puts it, "[I]s not that kind of losing a winning?"[44]

---

38. SKS 5, 306 / EUD, 314.
39. SKS 5, 306 / EUD, 315.
40. SKS 5, 306 / EUD, 314.
41. SKS 5, 306 / EUD, 314.
42. SKS 5, 308 / EUD, 316.
43. SKS 5, 309 / EUD, 317.
44. SKS 5, 309 / EUD, 317.

To be sure, the person no longer believes she has mastery over the external world: what once seemed open to conquest is now understood as the conqueror. In external things one "is not capable of anything at all,"[45] asserts Kierkegaard. And yet, if the self is to know itself in full, it also has to look *inward*. The clash between the first self and the deeper self, which concerns the person's orientation to phenomenal life, thus yields to the question of whether or not one can master one's internal life.

This question, according to Kierkegaard, is more like a riddle. How is one to overcome *oneself*? The very idea of "overcoming" presupposes the triumph of a stronger power over the resistance of a weaker power. With regard to the self, however, there is neither a stronger power nor a weaker power, for the self is struggling with itself. Therefore, he concludes, it cannot triumph *sensu stricto*.[46]

Kierkegaard knows this is a controversial claim. Human experience seems to suggest otherwise. For example, it is not unusual to hear of a person who, "tempted by worldly prestige, overcomes himself so that he no longer reaches out for it."[47] To such claims, however, Kierkegaard makes three points: (i) Talk about "overcoming oneself" is typically just a manner of speaking, which, in truth, refers to the mastery of some external temptation.[48] (ii) To say that one cannot overcome oneself is *not* to claim that human beings are in the power of evil; rather, it is to say that persons, while capable of *weathering* their internal trials and tribulations, are unable to conquer them once and for all.[49] (iii) Even when persons seem to overcome their own temptations, they can imagine greater ones *ad infinitum*. In this way, they come to realize the limits of their strength, to understand that, at

45. SKS 5, 310 / EUD, 318.
46. SKS 5, 310–11 / EUD, 318–19.
47. SKS 5, 311 / EUD, 319.
48. SKS 5, 311 / EUD, 319.
49. SKS 5, 311 / EUD, 320.

some point, their efforts to overcome themselves will fail.[50] Hence, in the end, it is clear that the internal state of human beings resembles the outer one: in both cases, they are "capable of nothing at all."[51]

Such claims, Kierkegaard acknowledges, might appear to be the "somber thoughts"[52] of a depressive. However, he insists that this realization is nothing short of joyous, for it "views life according to its perfection."[53] How so? First, detached from delusions of both external and internal control, the self receives an epiphany of God's constant presence—an epiphany that goes deeper than occasional prayers or even, Kierkegaard implies, the study of Scripture.[54] For now the self recognizes that, with every undertaking and in every moment, with every failure and with every success, God exists and is present. But this recognition is not an end in itself. It is a means to holiness: "We are not saying that knowing God or almost sinking into a dreaming admiration and a visionary contemplation of God is the *only* glorious thing to do . . ."[55] Rather, says Kierkegaard, the self's newfound awareness of God and of God's all-effective activity is "the condition for the sanctification of a human being by God's assistance and according to his intention."[56] To know oneself in one's own nothingness is to know God in truth, and to know God in truth is to be molded into a "new human being."[57]

By way of a conclusion, Kierkegaard offers a thought-experiment: might this radical dependence on God be understood in aesthetic

---

50. SKS 5, 311 / EUD, 320.
51. SKS 5, 311 / EUD, 320.
52. SKS 5, 311 / EUD, 320.
53. SKS 5, 312 / EUD, 321.
54. SKS 5, 312–13 / EUD, 322.
55. SKS 5, 316 / EUD, 325, my emphasis. Kierkegaard's use of the word "only" [alene] here suggests that he *does* see value in the contemplative life. However, like many other spiritual writers (particularly from the Devotio Moderna and Pietist movements), he ultimately places equal, if not greater, stress on the concrete expression of holiness—the so-called *vita activa*. This point will resurface in Chapter Five.
56. SKS 5, 316 / EUD, 325.
57. SKS 5, 316 / EUD, 325.

terms, that is, in terms of what *seems* to give life "the most beautiful meaning" amid a variety of theories about human self-actualization?[58] He answers "no." Moreover, he intensifies his preceding case. It is, he closes, "the first mystery of truth" that a human being "*is* nothing at all" and, for that reason, finds perfection only in needing God.[59]

In the end, then, both "To Need God" and *The Sickness unto Death* offer a conception of the self that necessitates spiritual growth. As has been seen, the self comes from God and is always in relationship with God. Yet, as an interplay of opposing forces, it is also susceptible to conflict from within and from without. In this vulnerability, moreover, it may very well stray from its origin. The sensual pleasures of earthly existence may become its sole focus, or, conversely, it may fail to engage life in full, preferring the virtual realities of, say, the Internet. But true happiness—and the complete flowering of freedom—remain ever possible. The self simply needs to journey back to God.

This conclusion indicates what, for Kierkegaard, is the condition of the self. But *how* is it supposed to remedy that condition? In other words, how is the self to make its way back to God? It is to that question, then, that this chapter now turns.

---

58. SKS 5, 316 / EUD, 325.
59. SKS 5, 316 / EUD, 325, my emphasis. Kierkegaard also uses this phrase—featuring the crucial verb, "to be" [*er*]—in an earlier passage. See SKS 5, 299 / EUD, 306. Here is another indication of his indebtedness to Meister Eckhart, Johannes Tauler, and others in the tradition of German Mysticism [*Deutsche Mystik*], as well as a sign that he is working with a metaphysical conception of the self. For a more focused discussion of this issue, see, once again, Christopher B. Barnett, "The Mystical Influence on Kierkegaard's Theological Anthropology," *Acta Kierkegaardiana* 6 (2013): 105–22. I especially deal with the *Deutsche Mystik* tradition on pp. 110–16.

Kierkegaard's Spiritual Itineraries

The presentation of a spiritual itinerary is a common and traditional feature of mystical literature. As Bernard McGinn points out, such itineraries are useful for a number of reasons.[60] First, they capture the idea that life is a kind of passage: people are not thrown into existence arbitrarily but, rather, are always moving progressively toward an ultimate goal. Second, itineraries are helpful organizing tools, giving structure to a process that can often seem disorienting. And, third, itineraries are common features of our everyday lives—consider, for example, an itinerary for a trip across Europe or even a daily planner—and so they provide a link between ordinary experience and spirituality. McGinn compares them to maps. Though they are not the terrain itself, they give persons a picture of how to navigate it.[61]

Kierkegaard was by no means averse to conceiving of spiritual growth in such terms. If anything, a number of itineraries are featured in his authorship. Below is a discussion of a few ways that Kierkegaard appropriates this motif, ranging from his categorization of life's evolving stages to his map of the journey through spiritual "sickness" or despair. As will be seen, faith is the endpoint, the goal, of spiritual maturation.

The Stages of Existence

One of the most recognized features of Kierkegaard's writings are his so-called "stages" or "spheres" of existence—a representation that seeks to track the self's ongoing development. For Kierkegaard, one's orientation to life is determined by the particular desires and interests with which one is occupied. For example, the habits and rhythms

60. Bernard McGinn, "Mystical Itineraries," in *The Essential Writings of Christian Mysticism*, ed. Bernard McGinn (New York: Modern Library, 2006), 149.
61. Ibid.

of one person's life might center on his favorite sports team, while another might derive her orientation from a certain ethical concern, say, from advocating on behalf of the environment. Though these sorts of life-views are exceedingly complex and numerous, Kierkegaard nevertheless argues that they can be grouped under one of three overarching categories—the aesthetic, the ethical, and the religious. These categories are not utterly discrete. For example, to inhabit a religious worldview is not to dispense with aesthetic concerns altogether.[62] It does mean, however, that such concerns are integrated into and transformed by the encompassing perspective of the religious. The reverse is also true. One's apparent religious interests can be nothing more than aestheticism, than superficiality.

The movement from the aesthetic through the ethical to the religious recalls the interaction between the first self and the deeper self discussed above. Just as the deeper self sought to draw the first self away from the allure of the external world, so do the stages of existence involve a progressive detachment from what is passing and an attachment to what abides. So, while the aesthete lives to get what she wants—be it material or spiritual gratification—the ethical person strives to get out of "the now" and to find a purpose in life. But this purpose, however noble, can also fasten the person to mundane affairs: a loving husband and father can think that he has "made it," simply by virtue of his decency. That such a self-conception is possible indicates the social character of his ethic. By doing what society asks of him (providing for his family, paying his taxes, and so on), he receives a sense of fulfillment.

But it is precisely here, notes Kierkegaard, that the religious begins to emerge. For, at some point, the ethical person must acknowledge the aporias, failures, and weaknesses that pervade every human life. This is an outlook that Kierkegaard, by way of a pseudonymous

62. This issue will be revisited in the following chapter.

character known only as "a priest in Jylland,"[63] puts forward at the end of *Either/Or*:

> If a person is sometimes in the right, sometimes in the wrong, to some degree in the right, to some degree in the wrong, who, then, is the one who makes that decision [about being right or wrong] except the person himself, but in the decision may he not again be to some degree in the right and to some degree in the wrong? . . . Is doubt to rule, then, continually to discover new difficulties, and is care to accompany the anguished soul and drum past experiences into it? . . . Then we have only the choice between being nothing in relation to God or having to begin all over again every moment in eternal torment. . . .[64]

Faced with this crisis, the Jylland pastor offers a simple "upbuilding" answer: in relation to God, no person is ever in the right. That is to say, one's ethical probity is only ever *relative*. One may be more or less right in any given situation, but, opposite an absolute standard, one cannot measure up.

Many persons might grant this point, but nevertheless wonder why it is upbuilding. According to the pastor, it is so in two ways. First, it replaces doubt with certainty. To see that one is ultimately in the wrong is to see that one's attempts at self-justification are futile. Second, its simplicity is therapeutic, liberating the person from ordinary patterns of thinking and relating and, in turn, providing newfound "energy to act."[65] More than anything else, however, it is a stark admission of humility—an admission that, in the end, the only one who truly comprehends life is God.

This rough overview of Kierkegaard's theory of the stages once again underlines his stress on the dynamism of human existence. All persons are capable of progressing toward spiritual fulfillment, which

---

63. SKS 3, 317 / EO2, 337, my translation. "Jylland," often referred to as "Jutland" in English, designates the large yet remote peninsula that constitutes the mainland of Denmark. It was pointed out in the previous chapter that Kierkegaard's father hailed from this area.
64. SKS 3, 325 / EO2, 346.
65. SKS 3, 331 / EO2, 352.

does not come through the annihilation of individual interests but, rather, through their appropriate refinement and integration. This is the task underlying all other tasks, and in it consists a lifetime of effort. Indeed, as will be seen below, Kierkegaard's writings make clear that even the religious life has its own stages of development.

The Levels of Religious Deepening

One of Kierkegaard's most celebrated works is his 1846 treatise *Concluding Unscientific Postscript to Philosophical Fragments*. It is a complex, even dizzying text, which has served as a major influence on modern philosophy and theology. And yet, perhaps nothing discloses its intentions so well as the pseudonym under which Kierkegaard issued it—Johannes Climacus.

John Climacus (ca. 570–649) was an Egyptian abbot, who penned one of the masterworks of the Christian spiritual tradition, *The Ladder of Divine Ascent*. The *Ladder* is divided into a series of chapters or "rungs," each of which has to do with a practice or virtue that leads to God—for example, the renunciation of the world, the attainment of "stillness," and the infusion of love. In this way, the *Ladder* recalls the paradoxical nature what has been referred to as "ascent literature." In order to *ascend* to God, one must *descend* into spiritual poverty.

It is on this point that the *Postscript* bears a resemblance to John's *Ladder*. For Kierkegaard's Climacus, no less than his monastic namesake, views the religious life as a process, which requires an ever-deepening recognition of the human being's humility before the divine. For him, then, it is not enough simply to arrive at the religious stage, to muster up a confession of Christian truth. On the contrary, one has to penetrate into its depths.

The first step, Climacus says, is coming to grips with what Christianity *is*. Too often people assume that it is a theory, which can be evaluated in neutral fashion alongside other metaphysical ideas about God, creation, and so on. But this is a twofold misunderstanding. First, it forgets that Christianity is primarily an "existence-communication,"[66] a *way*, which demands personal appropriation. Further, it tries to smooth over the "existence-contradiction"[67]—namely, that temporal activity determines one's relation to eternal happiness—underlying the Christian message. In both ways, Christianity stirs the passions of the one who would adhere to its teachings. It presents the alluring possibility of an eternal happiness, even as it shocks with the claim that the condition for this happiness is the entry of God into human history.

These two features are related but not identical. According to Climacus, one has to wrestle with the significance of an eternal happiness—a possibility that is characteristic of religion in general—before one can approach that which is uniquely Christian. The implication here is not that the former is easier, the latter harder. Rather, it is that the passionate struggle to relate to an eternal goal, which "is so strenuous for a human being that there is always sufficient task in it,"[68] is a *necessary* preparation for the reception of Christianity. Put differently, becoming a Christian is never as easy as simply assenting to a certain teaching or experiencing a certain feeling. It involves a journey through what Climacus terms "existential pathos" on the path toward faith in the incarnate God.

This journey is manifested in three stages. First, the person who truly strives for an eternal goal—or, in Climacus's terms, an absolute *telos*—comes to realize that this goal demands a corresponding action.

66. SKS 7, 346 / CUP1, 380.
67. SKS 7, 346 / CUP1, 380.
68. SKS 7, 506 / CUP1, 557.

Here he has in mind a monk or, say, a missionary, who gives up worldly comfort for the sake of his eternal happiness. This, notes Climacus, is a fitting and laudable response to something as momentous as unending beatitude. But there is a problem, and it leads to the second stage of inward deepening: the person's recognition that, in the end, it is not possible for an earthly, time-bound creature to perfectly relate to anything, much less to an absolute *telos*. Life is just too messy, too caught up in everyday affairs. For that reason, Climacus adds, this second stage is also marked by suffering, since what the religious person most wants (a perfect relation to God) is out of reach.

But who is responsible for this separation? Whose fault is it? The answer to this question pushes one further down the road of existential pathos. For now the person comes to accept her separation from eternal happiness as a matter of *guilt*. The notion of guilt here is not a matter of feeling "sorry" or of seeing oneself as a "bad" person. It has to do with an awareness that, at some point or in some way, *I* have failed to seek the highest good: a total commitment was required of me, but, in truth, I have given a partial response. Anything less than this admission is, in Climacus's view, a sign of spiritual dishonesty and, in turn, an additional mark of guilt. Thus the course through inward deepening culminates in a paradox: the more one is conscious of one's division from the absolute *telos*, the closer one presses to the divine. "The backward movement is nevertheless a forward movement inasmuch as immersing oneself in something means to go forward."[69]

For Climacus, it is at this point—and only at this point—that the person is ready for Christian teaching. Open to the hope for transcendence, but now painfully aware that it lies outside of *human*

69. SKS 7, 478–79 / CUP1, 527.

possibility, the person is vulnerable. This condition corresponds to the "nothingness before God" discussed above: the person is now in a state of receptivity to a "revelation from God that humans could not have discovered or invented using their own powers."[70] In turn, the preceding religious deepening is transformed into something new. Whereas before it was oriented to the person's *own* status as a religious individuality, now it is directed to another—namely, the figure of Jesus Christ.

Here, again, Kierkegaard's Climacus bears a resemblance to his monastic namesake: both recognize that the path of Christian spirituality must follow in the footsteps of Christ. That is precisely the greatness and the challenge of Christianity, which intensifies the paradoxical nature of the person's spiritual itinerary. This increased difficulty is not on account of any "works" on the person's part. After all, if one could work one's way to Christian perfection, then divine revelation would be superfluous. In a sense, then, all that is required is faith. *Faith is the final stage.* At the same time, however, the nature of faith, especially faith in Christ, brings trials of its own.

Climacus enumerates a number of incongruities that confront the believing person. First, faith concerns a *concrete* relationship with Jesus Christ, and this relation brings life to its highest pitch, since it understands earthly existence as the site where one's eternal happiness is decided. Second, the Christian claim that Christ is the God-man—the very basis for the person's relationship with Christ—lies beyond all historical knowledge. Consequently, the person has no more than *approximate* knowledge of that which he has placed at the center of life. Third, to believe that the eternal (God) can become historical (man) is to believe in "the absolute paradox."[71] In this

---

70. C. Stephen Evans, *Kierkegaard: An Introduction* (Cambridge: Cambridge University Press, 2009), 139.
71. SKS 7, 528 / CUP1, 580.

situation, the role of the intellect is to get out of the way, to use "the understanding so much that through it [one] becomes aware of the incomprehensible . . ."[72]

Faith, then, does not so much contravene reason as soar above it. But this ascension is not its own doing. At bottom, faith is a *submission*. It is an acceptance that eternal happiness—which the self desires but cannot win for itself—has been offered to it in and through the love of God, particularly as embodied in Jesus Christ. And from that acceptance the person is borne up, fulfilled by the divine.

This is a theme that Kierkegaard would return to in *The Sickness unto Death*—a text that might be viewed as a simplified (if not simple!) version of Climacus's understanding of religiousness. As will be seen, *The Sickness unto Death* also presents faith as the culmination of the self's spiritual journey, albeit in even more direct terms. Moreover, its greater concentration results in a different configuration. The passage now is just this—from despair to faith.

The Ladder of Despair

To this point several aspects of Kierkegaard's spirituality have emerged: (i) God is the origin of the human self, which, in turn, retains an intrinsic connection to its source; (ii) the self, however, is also drawn to earthly things, so much so that it may forget its divine origin and come to place its trust in what is, at best, fleeting and unreliable; (iii) this tension between the eternal and the temporal puts a great deal of strain on the self, whose dynamic and free nature must negotiate between a variety of competing interests; (iv) if the self is to find a true, enduring happiness, it must undertake a spiritual journey, which consists of an ever-deepening awareness of its limitations and,

72. SKS 7, 516 / CUP1, 568.

finally, its need for God; (v) this last point brings the self to the brink of *faith*—a surrender of one's life to the God revealed in Jesus Christ, who offers the condition for genuine existential fulfillment.

The Sickness unto Death does not so much add to this framework as compress it; moreover, it clarifies why persons fail to return to God, particularly due to the problem of despair or sin. As noted above, Kierkegaard issued the work under the pseudonym, Anti-Climacus—a signifier that at once links him to and separates him from Johannes Climacus. Like his predecessor, Anti-Climacus wants to account for how one can "climb" to God, albeit through a paradoxical collapse of one's sense of religious accomplishment and self-importance. Unlike his predecessor, however, Anti-Climacus writes as one who understands this process from the inside out. The prefix "Anti-" here indicates that he comes before, or is higher than, Johannes Climacus. While the latter seeks to grasp what Christianity is, Anti-Climacus *knows* it. He "considers himself to be a Christian on an extraordinarily high level,"[73] Kierkegaard notes.

This distinction accounts for the fastidious prose of *The Sickness unto Death*, which tends to resemble an instruction manual. And, in fact, this "exposition for upbuilding and awakening"[74] *is* a kind of manual. Much like the great Spanish mystic, John of the Cross, Anti-Climacus approaches the spiritual life in methodical fashion. This tactic ought not to suggest that individual appropriation and nuance lack importance. After all, a guidebook is only effective if *this* reader, applying the information to his peculiar circumstances, adheres to its directions. And yet, Anti-Climacus does imply that spiritual development proceeds according to certain universal

73. SKS 22, NB11:209 / JP 6, 6433.
74. This phrase comes from the book's full title: *The Sickness unto Death: A Christian Psychological Exposition for Upbuilding and Awakening.*

principles—an idea that, in turn, follows from his understanding of the nature of the self.

Recall that, for Anti-Climacus, the self is a combination of contrasting elements: the infinite and the finite, the eternal and the temporal, freedom and necessity. But these elements, in and of themselves, are not the self; rather, the self is that which consciously puts them in a relationship. For Anti-Climacus, then, the word "self" bears an active quality. It is something one *does*. And one can do it well or not so well, depending on how one "relates . . . to that which established the entire relation."[75] In other words, since the self comes from God, it cannot properly harmonize its contrary features without reference to its origin and its end, much like a car cannot be "tuned up" without taking into consideration its maker (a Hyundai is different than a Rolls Royce) or its purpose (moving heavy loads is different than racing).

But it is just here that problems arise. For the self, being free, can refuse to acknowledge this primordial relationship; it can refuse a "tune up." When this refusal happens, the self falls into despair. This is, in a sense, the starting point of *The Sickness unto Death*, which walks the reader, step-by-step, through various forms of despair. Thus it is a journey into the heart of darkness, though with an edifying purpose—to reveal the ways in which the self falls short of fulfillment so that, in turn, it can *receive* fulfillment in and from God.

Anti-Climacus analyzes despair in two overarching ways. The first way was alluded to earlier in this chapter—namely, as despair arises out of an imbalance among the self's constituent elements. Here it can become too wrapped up in time-bound, finite interests, or it can drift away, as it were, with the fantasies of the imagination. However, the second way is more complex and, according to Anti-Climacus, more

75. SKS 11, 129 / SUD, 13.

important. It views despair "within the category of consciousness."[76] C. Stephen Evans describes this approach as going "up the scale"[77]—a phrase that underlines the itinerary at the heart of Anti-Climacus's analysis, though, in this case, ascent signifies *distance* from God. The higher the despair, the farther from happiness.

The first form of conscious despair is, paradoxically, unconscious despair. This notion is not as strange as it might seem. Anti-Climacus is simply referring to the state in which the self lives without awareness of its nature and purpose. In this scenario, the self's despair is not so much a kind of rebellion as a kind of ignorance: it is so caught up in doing what is pleasant and avoiding what is unpleasant that it neglects "the absolute that a human being can be."[78] Anti-Climacus likens this state to a house:

> Imagine a house with a basement, first floor, and second floor planned so that there is or is supposed to be a social distinction between the occupants according to floor. Now, if what it means to be a human being is compared with such a house, then all too regrettably the sad and ludicrous truth about the majority of people is that in their own house they prefer to live in the basement.[79]

The challenge here is to awaken the person to his present condition and future potential: "he not only prefers to live in the basement—no, he loves it so much that he is indignant if anyone suggests that he move to the superb upper floor that stands vacant and at his disposal . . ."[80] This sort of attitude is fundamental to what Anti-Climacus identifies as a "pagan" worldview, which effectively reduces the self to an earthly function, institution, or role. But it has also insinuated itself into the lives of Christians, who, notes Anti-Climacus, have

76. SKS 11, 145 / SUD, 29.
77. Evans, *Kierkegaard*, 174.
78. SKS 11, 158 / SUD, 43.
79. SKS 11, 158 / SUD, 43.
80. SKS 11, 158 / SUD, 43.

fallen away from what their tradition expects of them. Theirs is "spiritlessness in the strictest sense."[81]

The next "rung" of despair is, naturally, conscious. That is to say, the self now understands its nature and purpose but also realizes that it has missed the mark. Conscious despair has two main forms. The first—and lower—form is "despair in weakness." This form has different levels of intensity, but each level shares a common trait: the self desires true happiness yet feels incapable of reaching it. This sort of despair culminates in what Anti-Climacus calls "despair over weakness." Here the self, "instead of definitely turning away from despair to faith and humbling [itself] under [its] weakness,"[82] becomes wrapped up in self-pity, sorry that it has failed to extricate itself from despair. But lurking behind this sense of helplessness is something more sinister—an "inclosing reserve,"[83] in which the self secretly applauds its superiority to those who are "shallow," even as it laments its failure to attain fulfillment. Anti-Climacus points out that such a person usually does quite well in the world—"a university graduate, husband, father, even an exceptionally competent public officeholder, a respectable father, pleasant company, very gentle to his wife"[84]—but this success is little more than a disguise. Deep down, the self of inclosing reserve is tormented, since its spiritual life is stuck in a vicious circle: the fulfillment for which it yearns will arrive if it will accept its weakness, but it is just this weakness that causes it to despair. It hates what it is; its despair is "not to will to be [itself]."[85]

This is not the case with the other main form of conscious despair, which Anti-Climacus identifies as "defiance." Whereas the previous self despairs over what it is not, this self errs by embracing what

81. SKS 11, 162 / SUD, 47.
82. SKS 11, 176 / SUD, 61.
83. SKS 11, 177-79 / SUD, 63–65.
84. SKS 11, 178 / SUD, 63–64.
85. SKS 11, 165 / SUD, 49.

it is—namely, a self in despair. Here the self uses its consciousness against itself. It is aware of its capacity for freedom and for imagination, but uses these faculties to separate it "from any relation to a power that has established it, or . . . from the idea that there is such a power."[86] In this way, the self becomes "its own master, absolutely its own master"[87] but with a cost: all it has is itself. That is to say, in placing itself at the center of the universe, the self is living a lie. It assumes that its activities bear "infinite interest and significance,"[88] when, in truth, they are products of a finite, time-bound creature and, therefore, lacking in permanence. What appears to be mastery, then, is closer to fiction: "it is easy to see that this absolute ruler is a king without a country,"[89] notes Anti-Climacus.

This defiance begins with a foppish sense of grandeur—the self dazzling with its ability to be whatever it feels like being—but terminates in a far darker place. For, eventually, limitations press upon the self. Some sort of failure creeps in, perhaps a physical debilitation or the loss of a loved one, and the self "feels itself nailed to this servitude."[90] At this point, the self completely turns against its maker and becomes "demonic."[91] It despises its limitation but, at the same time, situates this hatred at the core of its identity. In other words, it wills to be itself out of *spite* and "would rather rage against everything and be the wronged victim of the whole world and of all life"[92] than receive consolation. Thus self-hatred slips into the most profound form of self-love: not only does the self want to despair, but it wants to be *alone* with its despair. Its inclosing reserve is a "world *ex*-clusively for itself, a world where the self in despair is restlessly and

---

86. SKS 11, 182 / SUD, 68.
87. SKS 11, 183 / SUD, 69.
88. SKS 11, 183 / SUD, 69.
89. SKS 11, 183 / SUD, 69.
90. SKS 11, 184 / SUD, 70.
91. SKS 11, 185 / SUD, 72.
92. SKS 11, 185 / SUD, 72.

tormentedly engaged in willing to be itself."[93] Here, then, is the total breakdown of the self's relational structure and purpose.

This is, in one sense, the ultimate step on Anti-Climacus's ladder of despair. However, he concludes *The Sickness unto Death* with an essential addition: when the self despairs and, at the same time, understands itself to be in the presence of God, the result is *sin*. As he summarizes, "[S]in is intensified weakness or intensified defiance: sin is the intensification of despair."[94]

Anti-Climacus's word for "sin" is the Danish *Synd*, which is related to the German *Sünde*, also meaning "sin" or "misdeed." Both of these terms trace their origin to the German verb *sondern* ("to separate"), and, indeed, Anti-Climacus treats sin as a sharper, more decisive separation from authentic selfhood and from the self's source of being. This separation finds expression in particular acts—daily failures such as gossiping about a neighbor or more momentous ones such as theft—but Anti-Climacus insists that these are symptoms and not the disease. Thus his stress on sin is not to be confused with a kind of moralism, which places the greatest weight on polite behavior and so lapses into a superficial distinction between "the righteous" and "the wicked." On the contrary, for Anti-Climacus, sin is a "position" or a "state" in which the self is anchored. In this way, sin diametrically opposes the self's state of fulfillment, which, in his view, lies in a total anchoring in the power that established it. This state, as will be discussed below, is synonymous with "faith."

The self anchored to sin resists change in a number of ways. It can despair over sin, which, notes Anti-Climacus, has "the appearance of being something good" but is, in fact, "absorption in sin."[95] For such despair is the flipside of pride. The self believes itself to be superior

93. SKS 11, 186–87 / SUD, 73.
94. SKS 11, 191 / SUD, 77.
95. SKS 11, 222–23 / SUD, 111.

to sin, so that, when it sins, it grieves over what it has done. But this grief simply reinforces the "self-love that wants to be proud of itself, to be without sin."[96] Thus its sorrow indicates a "movement away from God," whereas it should have "humbly [thanked] God that he helped him to resist temptation . . . already much more than he deserved."[97]

In an even more intense form, the self's sinful resistance can be defined in relation to Christ, who mediates God's forgiveness of sins and, therefore, embodies "the inordinate concession" of the divine.[98] In Christ, God indicates "the staggering reality that a self has," for the union of Christ's human nature with his divine nature reveals that "God is man's goal and criterion."[99] Thus Christ extends the self's highest possibility—like many authors in the Christian spiritual tradition, Anti-Climacus sees *deification* as the self's ultimate destiny—though this extension also opens up a deeper dimension of despair:

> Sin was despair, the intensification was despair over sin. But now God offers reconciliation in the forgiveness of sin. Nevertheless, the sinner still despairs, and despair acquires a still deeper manifestation. . . . When the sinner despairs of the forgiveness of sins, it is almost as if he walked right up to God and said, "No, there is no forgiveness of sins, it is impossible . . ."[100]

Such a person, Anti-Climacus goes on, is *offended* by what Christ represents. This offense has a number of potential expressions—a subject that Kierkegaard, again via Anti-Climacus, returned to in *Practice in Christianity* (1850)—but all of them share a sense of insult and violation opposite Christ's person. To be offended is to not

96. SKS 11, 224 / SUD, 112.
97. SKS 11, 223–24 / SUD, 112.
98. SKS 11, 225 / SUD, 113.
99. SKS 11, 226 / SUD, 114.
100. SKS 11, 226 / SUD, 114.

believe in Christ. At its apex, however, offense not only *fails* to believe in Christ but positively declares Christianity "to be a lie and untruth."[101] Drawing on Christ's teaching,[102] Anti-Climacus states that this is the sin against the Holy Spirit, and it "makes Christ out to be an invention of the devil."[103] Here the Christian faith is rejected *in toto*.

Thus Anti-Climacus reaches the end of his spiritual ladder. It is, to be sure, heavy going, and more than a few readers have been put off by the labor. But Anti-Climacus insists that the path through the night of despair and sin is essential, since, paradoxically, it points the way to authentic human happiness. As Christ himself puts it, "[B]lessed is anyone who takes no offense at me" (Matt. 11:6). For Anti-Climacus, this is one of the most critical passages in the New Testament. If despair is sin, and if sin is offense, and if the removal of offense leads to blessedness, then blessedness is the opposite of offense. But what, exactly, is blessedness? Anti-Climacus's answer is simple: it is *faith*. To have faith is to overcome the problem of despair/sin, and thus faith is the pivotal moment of the self's spiritual journey.

It was mentioned earlier that, for Johannes Climacus, faith is the final stage of religious deepening. And now it is clear Anti-Climacus has a similar view, though he arrives at it in different fashion. Faith, then, has emerged as a central feature of Kierkegaardian spirituality, representing the climactic step on human being's *reditus* to God. Hence, before closing this chapter, a more thorough investigation of faith is necessary.

101. SKS 11, 236 / SUD, 125.
102. See Matt. 12:30-32, Mark 3:28-30, and Luke 12:8-10.
103. SKS 11, 242 / SUD, 131.

Faith

With its roots in Latin verb *fidere* ("to trust"), "faith" is an inherently relational term. It concerns a way of knowing, which does not rely on empirical proof or logical verification but, rather, on a resolution to trust in someone. Such a decision is not necessarily irrational—for example, Anti-Climacus's analysis of despair makes a compelling case for the benefits of faith—but it is, at the same time, more than a formula or a theory. Faith involves the whole person, her deepest longings and hopes. In short, it is a *spiritual* quality, which, in Christian terms, encourages the person "to relax into the surprise of being loved by God."[104]

Kierkegaard's authorship presupposes and builds on this general understanding of faith, culminating, once again, with *The Sickness unto Death*. As has been suggested, Anti-Climacus views the fundamental divide in the spiritual life as "sin/faith."[105] That is to say, he does not see sin as opposed to righteousness or to virtue; instead, he contrasts it with faith. This approach follows from his understanding of sin as a condition, rather than as a deed. The sinner is one who, in despair and before God, either does not want to be oneself or does want to be oneself. Thus sin is, at bottom, a broken self-relationship—the self's failure to be what it is supposed to be.

As the opposite of sin, faith is a state too. It is not a blind wish, a virtuous action, or a mere creedal assent. On the contrary, it is a way of being, in which the self relates properly to itself and to its maker. As Anti-Climacus puts it, "[This is] the formula for the state in which there is no despair at all: in relating itself to itself and in willing to be itself, the self rests transparently in the power that established it. This formula in turn . . . is the definition of faith."[106] On this reading,

---

104. Michael Paul Gallagher, "Faith," in *The New Westminster Dictionary of Christian Spirituality*, ed. Philip Sheldrake (Louisville: Westminster John Knox, 2005), 297–98.
105. SKS 11, 242 / SUD, 131.

virtue proceeds from faith but is not identical to faith, just as vice proceeds from despair but is not identical to despair. Faith, then, has major ramifications for the ethical life and, for that reason, is "an excellence that makes a self genuinely human."[107] And yet, faith itself is *not* a work. As C. Stephen Evans notes, "The claim being made is that faith as genuine selfhood cannot be achieved simply through autonomous moral striving."[108] To have faith is not to take possession; it is to let be.

This point sheds light on one of the more peculiar and intriguing turns of phrase in Kierkegaard's authorship—namely, the claim that faith is a "transparent rest" in God. According to Paul Cruysberghs, this idea involves the self's recognition of its dividedness, as well as a humble acknowledgement that, left to its own devices, it is simply "unclear"[109] about its nature and purpose. Such honesty, Cruysberghs goes on, is tantamount to resting transparently in God, for the self has taken account of its own failures and limitations and, in turn, been unconcealed before its founding power.[110] This process of unconcealment is precisely what makes faith so rare in the world; it is why Anti-Climacus insists that faith never arrives as "a matter of course."[111] Salvation may be easy—since it is accomplished by God—but faith requires human cooperation and, with it, human struggle.[112] As Kierkegaard puts it in an 1850 journey entry, "To

---

106. SKS 11, 242 / SUD, 131.
107. Evans, *Kierkegaard*, 182.
108. Ibid.
109. Paul Cruysberghs, "Transparency to Oneself and to God," in *At være sig selv nærværende: Festskrift til Niels Jørgen Cappelørn*, ed. Joakim Garff, Ettore Rocca, and Pia Søltoft (Copenhagen: Kristeligt Dagblads Forlag, 2010), 138–39.
110. Ibid., 137–38.
111. SKS 11, 173 / SUD, 58.
112. Simon Podmore, who has written a great deal about the theme of "spiritual trial" in Kierkegaard's authorship, notes that the "abyss between the human and the divine" necessitates that the self's "resting place" in God is always tied to a spiritual restlessness, which must be "overcome through moments of dying to self-will in the longing to unite with the will of God" (Simon D. Podmore, *Struggling with God: Kierkegaard and the Temptation of Spiritual Trial*

be made well with the aid of Christianity is not the difficulty; the difficulty is in becoming sick to some purpose. If you are sick in this way, Christianity comes with matchless ease, just as it is incomparably easy for the starving person to be interested in food."[113] The "food" is God and salvation, received in and through the hunger of faith.

Here, again, Kierkegaard's robust and textured understanding of faith is evident. It is a term that, so to speak, does a great deal of work for him, bringing together a number of key themes in the history of Christian spirituality. This richness, so dense on a historical and theological level, is one reason why this book will turn to Kierkegaard's depictions of "icons of faith" in its second half. For Kierkegaard's literary touch renders beautiful what analysis would complicate.

At the same time, however, it is worth pointing out that the concept of "transparent rest" has resonances that, in turn, bring out the import of faith. One might start with the expression itself. Anti-Climacus's exact phrase for "rests transparently" is *grunder gjennemsigtigt*—literally, "is grounded in a see-through manner." A "ground" (whether in an electrical circuit or in an argument) is a foundation; it is that upon which something else is based. Thus the verb "to ground" means to place something on, or to keep something in contact with, a foundation. Likewise, in everyday life, it is said that a person is "grounded" when she remains in touch with her

---

[Cambridge: James Clarke & Co., 2013], 216). These "moments" are analogous to the notion of spiritual journey articulated here, though Podmore is, perhaps, more reluctant than I to emphasize faith as a resolution of the angst intrinsic to Christian spirituality. As he writes, "Full consummation of…[the] transfiguration of the self as Spirit, resting transparently grounded in God…may remain an eschatological vanishing point for those who, for now, struggle to hold on to God in the darkness of night" (Ibid., 266). And yet, it is worth adding that Kierkegaard's "icons of faith," which will be discussed in Chapters Four and Five, do not only depict faith's trials but also its joyful love. In short, Kierkegaard wants to hold together what (to draw on Podmore's language) can be seen as the desolation and consolation of faith.

113. SKS 23, NB19:25 / JP 2, 1137.

origins, as when a highly successful person (say, a president or a billionaire) remains humble by recalling the more modest conditions of her childhood. Such a person might be described as "transparent," because the trappings of achievement have not covered over who she truly is. One can *see through* the external pomp and circumstance to the interior person, who retains a connection to and a reliance on that which (or those who) initiated, endowed, and sustained her existence. Moreover, this foundational orientation continues to guide the way she interacts with the world, despite the distractions and responsibilities of the present day.

This sort of meaning is borne out by Anti-Climacus's analysis of the self. As has been seen, he views the self as a created synthesis of finite and infinite elements. Though good in and of themselves, these constituents can fall into disorder and lead to despair, unless they are harmonized through the transparent rest of faith. In faith, the person receives the benefits of remaining true to who he really is—namely, a creature whose origin is from God. Consequently, he will not let finite matters or imaginative ideas obscure the basic trust he has in his creator. In fact, this basic trust guides him through life, nurturing a sense of life's intrinsic value, even as it cultivates a desire for the supernatural reconciliation of earthly injustice and sorrow.

The person of faith, then, is *grounded* in God. Her self-knowledge, as well as the knowledge through which she understands the world, "rests" in the very foundation of being. In this way, she sees and wills as God sees and wills, and faith becomes nothing less than a state of happiness.

It may seem peculiar that Anti-Climacus's conception of faith makes no specific reference to an ecclesial creed or a biblical declaration. He by no means rules out such a profession of faith, but nevertheless presents something more basic, more intimate—an approach that hints at another echo in his notion of "resting transparently" in God. It has been pointed out that Kierkegaard was familiar with a number of the masterworks of Christian spirituality, particularly those favored by the Pietist movement, including Catholic mystics such as Johannes Tauler and Protestant writers such as Johann Arndt. In those works—but especially in Tauler, the great disciple of Meister Eckhart—Kierkegaard encountered the idea of the "ground of the soul" [*Grund der Seele*]. The "ground" is, as it were, the divine seed left in the human being at creation. Thus it is not put there by the human being, nor can human sin eradicate it. Rather, it is the part of the human being that bears the image of God (Gen. 1:27). The ground, then, is what distinguishes human beings from other animals—one might think of it in terms of "intellect" or, like Kierkegaard, in terms of self-reflexive relationality—and, through it, each person has the potential to unite with God.

But how, exactly, is this reunion possible? For Tauler, as for Eckhart, one returns to the ground of the soul by giving up or "detaching" from whatever blocks one's attention to it. Such distractions can range from basic needs such as eating and drinking to concerns over pleasure, power, status, and even holiness. Moreover, the intellect itself can be a distraction, if it is allowed to fashion idols for itself and to grow satisfied with fantasies. Thus detachment is the process by which one cuts away from the things of the world and becomes *grounded*. Without it, one's relationship with the divine is unclear—indeed, lacks transparency—muddied as it is by the disturbances and diversions of earthly life. To refuse to detach is, to express it in Anti-Climacus's terms, to remain in the grip of despair.

The implication here is not that the so-called *Deutsche Mystik* of Eckhart and Tauler stands as a direct or even principal influence on *The Sickness unto Death*. It is to say that Anti-Climacus's understanding of faith is not at all alien to the Christian tradition but, rather, bears a notable resemblance to the thought of other Christian spiritual writers, particularly those (like Tauler) with whom he had a degree of familiarity. Put more strongly, one could justifiably group Anti-Climacus in with a number of Christian authors—ranging from Paul of Tarsus to John of the Cross—who recognize the spiritual life as a progressive "surrendering of deeply imbedded resistances that allows the sacred within gradually to reveal itself as a simple fact."[114] On this understanding, the human being is never really separate from God, and, so, the goal of spirituality is to peel away the obscuring cataract of separation. For Anti-Climacus, faith is the means to this end, and its outcome is to understand that one lives, moves, and has one's being in God (Acts 17:28). Martin Laird, though writing in a broader context, manages to sum up Anti-Climacus's view nicely:

> We might liken the depths of the human to the sponge in the ocean. The sponge looks without and sees ocean; it looks within and sees ocean. The sponge is immersed in what at the same time flows through it. The sponge would not be a sponge were this not the case. . . . [Likewise] the more we realize we are one with God the more we become ourselves, just as we are, just as we were created to be. The Creator is outpouring love, the creation, the love outpoured.[115]

As the sponge rests in the ocean, so, for Anti-Climacus, does the person of faith rest in God—suffused with the divine presence, but authentically himself, since he has come to recognize his true nature and end.

If the preceding stands as the *content* of Kierkegaard's conception of the self and its journey back to God, the *form* of Kierkegaard's ideas remains to be seen. In the coming chapters, we will look at Kierkegaard's "icons of faith"—his depictions of those figures who embody the life of faith. First, however, it is necessary to establish

---

114. Martin Laird, O. S. A., *Into the Silent Land: A Guide to the Christian Practice of Contemplation* (Oxford: Oxford University Press, 2006), 8.
115. Ibid., 17.

the basis for this approach. After all, Kierkegaard is a well-known (if often misunderstood) critic of "the aesthetic," and so attention to the various "pictures" populating his writings might seem strange, even erroneous. Thus a discussion of Kierkegaard's understanding of the relation between the religious and the aesthetic, taken up in the next chapter, is very much in order.

3

Kierkegaard and the Aesthetics of the Icon

The previous two chapters have established (i) that Kierkegaard was a kind of spiritual writer and (ii) that his theological anthropology, with its overarching theme of "exit and return," treats human life as a journey back to God—a journey that culminates in faith, which grounds the human being in God and, in turn, brings fulfillment. Thus far, the analysis has been more descriptive than argumentative; however, this chapter will address one of the classic debates in Kierkegaard scholarship, namely, the degree to which Kierkegaard sought to drive a wedge between aesthetics and religion. In doing so, it will pave the way for an exploration of the various figures, or icons, that exemplify Kierkegaardian spirituality.

That this issue invites controversy is, in one sense, one of the great ironies of intellectual history. After all, Kierkegaard was not only a lover of the arts—famously, he was said to have never missed a performance of Mozart's *Don Giovanni* at Copenhagen's Royal Theater[1]—but he is widely held to be the Danish language's finest

---

1. Joakim Garff, *Søren Kierkegaard: A Biography*, trans. Bruce H. Kirmmse (Princeton, NJ: Princeton University Press, 2005), 121.

prose stylist. As Joakim Garff puts it, "[W]hat Danish writer had ever produced anything so fertile and prodigious?"[2] And this is to say nothing of Kierkegaard's remarkable impact on twentieth-century art, from the films of Carl Theodor Dreyer to the music of Samuel Barber to the paintings of Mark Rothko. W. H. Auden—the outstanding English poet, and himself an admirer of Kierkegaard—once acclaimed the "brilliantly poetic" nature of Kierkegaard's writings, though he quickly added that Kierkegaard was not so much a poet as a "preacher, an expounder and defender of Christian doctrine and Christian conduct."[3] In this distinction lies much of the disagreement regarding Kierkegaard's relation to aesthetics.[4]

Auden's assertion that Kierkegaard's poetic sensibilities ultimately yield to a more pronounced, more severe Christian vein finds plenty of corroboration in the secondary literature. A well-known example of this tendency lies in the work of George Pattison, who traces the rift back to Kierkegaard's 1846 treatise *A Literary Review*. In that work, Kierkegaard chides "the present age" for its embrace of reflection—its tendency to reject authority and tradition in favor of a mindset critical of everything but the individual's self-interest. Consequently, social institutions and relations have been reduced

---

2. Ibid., 334.
3. W. H. Auden, "Presenting Kierkegaard," in *The Living Thoughts of Kierkegaard*, ed. W.H. Auden (Bloomington: Indiana University Press, 1952), 3.
4. Here "aesthetics" is meant in a general sense—namely, as the study of or reflection on objects of perception. Indeed, the word "aesthetics" itself comes from the Greek term *aisthanesthai* ("to perceive"), although, through Plato and others, it has taken on the additional significance of dealing with perceptions that, in particular, are deemed beautiful or sublime. Kierkegaard seems to have taken on both usages. For him, "aesthetics" or "the aesthetic" do concern what one can see, touch, or hear. Such perceptions are simply part of the data that make up human life, and, so, as it is put in *Either/Or*, "[T]he esthetic is not evil but the indifferent" (SKS 3, 165 / EO 2, 169). At the same time, however, these perceptions—especially beautiful, pleasing ones—can wield an influence over one's life, drawing one to this or to that end. It is in this sense that, for Kierkegaard, the aesthetic can be dangerous or beneficial. The task of this chapter is to trace out this dialectic, with particular focus on the aesthetic concept of "image."

to instruments of utility. What once stirred the passions of people—whether God or country or love—have become objectively meaningless. According to Pattison, this insight compels Kierkegaard to divorce the religious from the aesthetic, even as both emerge as potential escapes from the abyss of modernity. For art's redemption is nothing more than a whimsy, especially in an epoch of reflection, when the aesthetic preoccupation with *form* has been detached from any meaningful *content*. Thus art, too, has succumbed to the present age: it titillates but does not elevate. As Pattison goes on to explain:

> [T]he aesthetic may no longer be regarded as a legitimate stage on the path to a religious awakening. To stay with aesthetic is to refuse the religious. . . . Although reflection has in one sense destroyed the possibility of great art, an age that fails to choose faith with the decisiveness of inward passion is . . . an "aesthetic" age. The aesthetic has become the inauthentic.[5]

The only hope for the individual, then, is to seek "the religious in the absolute interiority of the self."[6] Even concrete ethical striving in the world has become unrecognizable, *form-less*.

Pattison tenders his reading with somber understanding, adding that Kierkegaard's critique of modern art has served to shape its consciousness. In fact, as he sees it, the "death of art" has come to give an almost religious mission to the contemporary artist.[7] But other commentators are not as sympathetic with Kierkegaard's vision. Perhaps the sharpest critique of this sort was issued by the eminent Swiss Catholic thinker Hans Urs von Balthasar. Critical of modern theology's preoccupation with logic and ethics at the expense of beauty, Balthasar commenced one of the breakthrough theological

5. George Pattison, "Art in an Age of Reflection," in *The Cambridge Companion to Kierkegaard*, eds. Alastair Hannay and Gordon D. Marino (Cambridge: Cambridge University Press, 1998), 97.
6. Ibid., 96.
7. Ibid., 98.

projects of the twentieth century—his seven-volume work *The Glory of the Lord* [*Herrlichkeit*]. Its aim, taken as a whole, is "to complement the vision of the true and the good with that of the beautiful" and, in turn, to "show how impoverished Christian thinking has been by the growing loss of this perspective which once strongly informed theology."[8] For Balthasar, this is indeed an urgent task. Today, he says, beauty has become "a mere appearance" in a "world of interests,"[9] and thus its fate is to be either exploited or forgotten. But beauty's loss is also humanity's. As Balthasar goes on to explain, "In a world without beauty . . . the good also loses its attractiveness, the self-evidence of why it must be carried out. Man stands before the good and asks himself why *it* must be done and not rather its alternative, evil."[10] This diagnosis bears a theological prescription—namely, a return to the *form* of divine revelation. For it is only through form that beauty shines and "the ray of the Unconditional breaks through, casting a person down to adoration and transforming him into a believer and a follower."[11]

With this concern established, Balthasar turns to a genealogical account of how beauty was torn from the fabric of Western society. It is, for him, a theological story, which has its origins in the Protestant Reformation in general and in Martin Luther's teaching in particular. For Balthasar, Luther's insistence on "God's absolute veiledness"—an emphasis derived from his distaste for Neoplatonic and Thomist versions of the *analogia entis*—results in a rejection of "[e]very form which man tries to impose on revelation in order to achieve an overview that makes comprehension possible . . ."[12] One can no

8. Hans Urs von Balthasar, *The Glory of the Lord: A Theological Aesthetics*, vol. 1, trans. Erasmo Leiva-Merikakis (San Francisco: Ignatius Press, 1982), 9.
9. Ibid., 18.
10. Ibid., 19.
11. Ibid., 32.
12. Ibid., 47.

longer look at a created form—say, a sunset or a sleeping child—and ascertain a likeness to the divine. In this way, Luther sunders nature and grace and, with it, the aesthetic and the religious.

It is at this point that Balthasar begins to attend to Kierkegaard, who, in his view, reaps what Luther had sown centuries before. Indeed, by the nineteenth century, art had been totally uncoupled from its relationship with theology, freeing the Romantics to deem aesthetics the "supreme value of any worldview."[13] From there it was but a short step to the aesthetic nihilism of Friedrich Nietzsche—a development that, according to Balthasar, Kierkegaard foresaw and opposed. Realizing that modern aesthetics was "frivolous, merely curious and self-indulgent," Kierkegaard fired back with an emphasis on "inwardness and religious subjectivity."[14] But this response lacked comprehensiveness, and it led Kierkegaard to deepen—rather than to overcome—the chasm between aesthetics and religion. As Balthasar explains,

> Kierkegaard can no longer achieve a meeting of religion and aesthetics. He is impelled to use the concept of "the aesthetic" to stake out and define a basic attitude which, for the Christian, is unacceptable . . . thereby eradicating from theology all traces of an aesthetic attitude. . . . [T]his enthusiastic disjunction robs man, as it were from within, of all joy in the aesthetic. . . .[15]

Thus Kierkegaard stands as both an accomplice to, and a victim of, Luther's theology. Even worse, the Dane's influence on twentieth-century ideas worked to popularize Lutheran thinking. As Balthasar puts it, "The Kierkegaard revival in various ways had an anti-aesthetic effect on theology."[16]

13. Ibid., 49.
14. Ibid., 51.
15. Ibid., 49.
16. Ibid., 51.

In light of Pattison's and Balthasar's analyses, it would seem unlikely that a positive appraisal of aesthetics can be developed from Kierkegaard's oeuvre. His ostensible opposition of the aesthetic and the religious, not to mention the fact that he himself never penned a proper treatise on the subject, appears to quell any such enterprise. The goal of this chapter, however, is to argue to the contrary. Specifically, I will show that an "aesthetics of the icon" is implicit in Kierkegaard's own copious employment of aesthetic imagery. Rather than rupturing the two spheres, he has a dialectical view of the matter: aesthetic imagery can function either in the manner of icons or in that of idols.

This point will be established in three ways. First, the concept of "image" or "picture" [*Billede*] in Kierkegaard's authorship will be explored. As will be seen, Kierkegaard uses this term in a variety of contexts, imbuing it with both negative and positive significance. Next it will be argued that this dialectical usage of *Billede* informs his orientation toward the aesthetic in general. An aesthetic image either can draw one into its own ambit, or it can deflect one to something higher—indeed, to godliness. The upshot of this dialectic is a potential integration of the aesthetic and the religious in Kierkegaard's thinking. For inasmuch as the aesthetic brings one to seek the religious in one's concrete existence, Kierkegaard not only applauds it but *employs* it. Finally, Kierkegaard's understanding of the relationship between aesthetics and religion will be illustrated by way of the thought of the French philosopher Jean-Luc Marion. In particular, it will be pointed out that Marion's distinction between the idol and the icon—whereby the former aims to absorb the gaze of the observer, the latter to redirect it—can shed light on the multitude of "pictures" populating Kierkegaard's writings. To be sure, there are idols, but Kierkegaard also fashions icons of faith. In this way—and with a measure of irony—he actually fulfills Balthasar's demand for attention to the *form* of Christian existence.

The Concept of *Billede* in Kierkegaard's Authorship

The term *Billede*, meaning "picture," "image," or "reflection," occurs with regularity in Kierkegaard's authorship. In one form or another, it appears more than three hundred times in Kierkegaard's writings, published as well as unpublished. Moreover, its usage spans his corpus, turning up as early as 1838's *From the Papers of One Still Living* and as late as 1855's articles in *Fædrelandet*. An exhaustive analysis of *Billede*, then, is neither possible nor desirable in this setting. Instead, a few representative instances of the term will be examined, showing how Kierkegaard employs it in a variety of contexts and senses.

An early and striking example of Kierkegaard's use of *Billede* occurs in the first part of *Either/Or*—namely, in its final section, "The Seducer's Diary." The story's antihero, the aptly termed Johannes the Seducer, has followed his *objet d'amour* into a Copenhagen shop. Her name is Cordelia, a mere girl at seventeen years of age. Johannes watches as she makes her way through the store, fondling the items for sale with blissful caprice. In order to remain unnoticed, he stands across the room, eyeing Cordelia in a large mirror mounted on a wall. The mirror, he notes, is at once his rival and collaborator. Its seizure of her image is akin to contemplation, to devotion. However, it cannot keep her image all to itself; rather, it must deliver it to others, who are not so unfortunately constituted:

Unhappy mirror, which assuredly can grasp her image [*Billede*] but not her; unhappy mirror, which cannot secretly hide her image in itself, hide it from the whole world, but can only disclose it to others as it now does to me. What torture if a human being were fashioned that way.[17]

Indeed, Johannes is not fashioned that way. He compares Cordelia's figure to the voluptuousness of a piece of fruit. He can, he says, *feel* her with his eyes. And, accordingly, he aims to consume her. As he puts it, "[E]verything will be relished in slow mouthfuls; she is picked out, she will be gathered."[18]

It is noteworthy here that Johannes, the aesthete, only interacts with an *image* of Cordelia. Kierkegaard makes this point especially clear by using the mirror as a mediator between the two characters. He does not relate to her as a three-dimensional human being but, rather, as a two-dimensional reflection. And this reflection consumes him as much as he wants to consume it—a detail that hints at why Johannes has been called a "pitiable creature,"[19] despite his blatant exploitation of others. For "he is incapable of a real meeting, a real encounter with another person, incapable of dealing with a situation of mutual responsibility."[20] In this sense, Johannes is an antiquated, but no less authentic, version of a pornography addict. For him, image and reality have been confused; or more precisely, the aesthetic as such has become his life. Even when he acts within the continuum of the real world, he remains imprisoned in his own world of fantasies, for only fantasies are capable of arousing and gratifying him.[21] Pattison sums up Kierkegaard's point well: "What he is showing is what happens when one tries to base life on an 'image'."[22]

The Seducer's aesthetic attitude terminates in sexual abuse, but elsewhere Kierkegaard points out that the lure of the image can corrupt in different ways. Insofar as it effects a break with the real world, aestheticism is like a mold that spoils whatever it touches, be

---

17. SKS 2, 305 / EO 1, 315.
18. SKS 2, 306 / EO 1, 317, my translation.
19. George Pattison, *Kierkegaard and the Crisis of Faith: An Introduction to his Thought* (London: SPCK, 1997), 76.
20. Ibid.
21. SKS 2, 296 / EO 1, 306.
22. Pattison, *Kierkegaard*, 76.

it sex, politics, or religion. Kierkegaard highlights this latter point in his 1850 work, *Practice in Christianity*, particularly in the sixth exposition of the section entitled "From on High He Will Draw All to Himself." There Kierkegaard's pseudonym, Anti-Climacus, explores the ambiguity of "observing" an object, as when "one shows a painting to a person and asks him to observe it."[23] On the one hand, he notes, the observer must come close to the object of observation, so as to get a better look at it. On the other hand, the observer must also remain "infinitely distant" from it, since "by observing I go into the object (I become objective) but I leave myself or go away from myself (I cease to be subjective)."[24] For Anti-Climacus, this dialectic captures precisely what is wrong with Christendom in the present age. The preacher stands in the pulpit and makes "observations,"[25] but neglects to emphasize that "it is Christian truth that is observing me, whether I am doing what it says I should do."[26]

This is also, he goes on, the danger with Christian art. Though he admits that he cannot "pass judgment" on all artists, Anti-Climacus gives two main reasons why he could never paint "the image" [*Billedet*] of Jesus Christ.[27] First, in order to paint Christ's image, he would have to secure a certain amount of "leisure,"[28] allowing him to shirk what Christ asks of his day-to-day life so that, instead, he could paint a picture. Second, he worries that the finished product—the painting of Christ as such—would distort the meaning of the religious life. For in the painting "the artist admired himself, and everybody

23. SKS 12, 227 / PC, 233.
24. SKS 12, 227–28 / PC, 234–35.
25. Here Anti-Climacus is making a rather unsubtle reference to Jakob Peter Mynster's 1846 book *Observations on the Doctrines of the Christian Faith* [*Betragtninger over de christelige Troeslærdomme*]. At that time, Mynster was Bishop of Zealand and a prominent Danish intellectual. As is well known, he eventually would become one of the principal objects of Kierkegaard's criticism during the latter's so-called "attack upon Christendom" of 1854–55.
26. SKS 12, 228 / PC, 234.
27. SKS 12, 246–47 / PC, 254–55.
28. SKS 12, 246 / PC, 255, my translation.

admired the artist."[29] In this scenario, the person reflected in the image has been forgotten, eclipsed by the image itself. As Anti-Climacus explains,

> [T]he beholder looked at the picture [*Billedet*] in the role of an art expert: whether it is a success, whether it is a masterpiece, whether the play of colors is right, and the shadows, whether blood looks like that, whether the suffering expression is artistically true – but the invitation to imitation he did not find.[30]

Here Anti-Climacus reiterates the trouble with Johannes the Seducer, albeit in a Christian context. The person who views Christ's image as an end in itself, who allows the *picture* to occupy her more than the real thing, has abstracted the aesthetic from the religious and, in turn, transformed it into an idol.

Significantly, this critique is not limited to artists or to the bourgeois aesthetes of Christendom. In an 1850 journal entry, Kierkegaard chides the Moravian Brethren—with whom, as has been mentioned, he had both familial ties and theological affinities—for "gazing at Christ's suffering" rather than accentuating the "imitation" of Christ.[31] Thus he suggests that it is not enough to celebrate the Passion of Christ with liturgical and artistic pieces—a customary and, at times, extravagant feature of Moravian piety, perhaps best captured by "Christ Scourged," a masterpiece of the great Moravian painter, Johann Valentin Haidt (1700–80). Instead the religious in general, and Christianity in particular, are to be distinguished by their concrete realization in one's own life. To put it in Anti-Climacus's terms, art may produce people who *admire* Christianity, but admiration is beside the point: "Only the imitator is the true Christian."[32]

29. SKS 12, 247 / PC, 255.
30. SKS 12, 247–48 / PC, 255–56.
31. SKS 23, NB20:78 / JP 2, 1874, my translation.

It is clear, then, that Kierkegaard's writings treat *Billede* as a dangerous concept. Enticed to gaze at an image, one can—almost like Narcissus—fall in love with what is not real and come to die, in spirit if not in body. But elsewhere Kierkegaard takes a different tack. Particularly in his upbuilding discourses, he is inclined to describe certain biblical heroes as "images." Indeed, he does not just *call* them images but uses his pen to sketch them in rich, pictorial language.

A good early example of this tendency turns up in "Patience in Expectancy," the second address from 1844's *Two Upbuilding Discourses*. There Kierkegaard discusses Anna, the aged prophetess who witnessed the presentation of the infant Jesus to the Temple authorities in Jerusalem.[33] What strikes Kierkegaard about Anna, however, is not so much her presence at this momentous event as her many years as a widow, during which she apparently remained devoted both to her husband and to God. As he envisions it, where another might have sought solace in "multifarious expectancies,"[34] Anna has passed her long life in quiet fortitude, faithful to her husband's memory and hopeful that God will reunite them—and all things—in eternity. Thus Kierkegaard goes on:

> My listener, let your thoughts dwell on this venerable woman, [who] . . . stands as the eternal's young fiancée. This tranquillity in her eyes that nevertheless is expectant, this gentleness that is reconciled to life and nevertheless is expectant . . . beyond flowering, nevertheless still vigorous, forsaken nevertheless not withered, childless nevertheless not barren, bent with years and stooped nevertheless not broken—a widow, nevertheless betrothed, "she is in silence" with her expectancy.[35]

Here he breaks off, adding that this "picture" [*Billede*] of Anna is "beautiful," so much so that "one could sit and grow old

32. SKS 12, 248 / PC, 256.
33. See Luke 2:36-38.
34. SKS 5, 212 / EUD, 211.
35. SKS 5, 212 / EUD, 211–12.

contemplating [it], powerless to tear oneself away from it."[36] It is, in fact, "the object of contemplation"[37] [*Betragtningens Gjenstand*] for those who rightly understand that life is replete with peril and disappointment but not bereft of hope. In fact, the *Billede* of Anna is more than a picture of a human being; it is a reflection of the eternal. As Kierkegaard explains, "[T]he object of expectancy, the more glorious and precious it is, [forms] the expectant person in its own likeness, because a person resembles what he loves with his whole soul."[38]

With his evocative prose, not to mention his mystically tinged language of "contemplation," Kierkegaard effectively treats Anna as an icon—that is to say, as an image of the sacred. Moreover, he invites his "listener" to do the same, to see in his rendering of Anna a picture of patient expectancy. But this *Billede* is not to be an end in itself. The one who properly contemplates it does so in order to reproduce Anna's virtue in one's own life. After all, this is an *upbuilding* discourse. And it is Kierkegaard's painting of Anna that occasions the upbuilding.

Indeed, for Kierkegaard, Christian faith has a kind of form. It does not issue in just any appearance but, rather, bears certain contours and features. That is not to say, of course, that it is reducible to a particular manner of dress or single way of living. Nor is it to forget that even an ideal form—such as Christ's—can be approached in the wrong fashion. Nevertheless, Kierkegaard insists that the image of *worship* signifies the content of faith, including, paradoxically, the very object of faith. As he writes,

> In truth, to be able to worship is what makes the [human being's] invisible glory superior to the rest of creation. The pagan was not aware

36. SKS 5, 212 / EUD, 212.
37. SKS 5, 213 / EUD, 212.
38. SKS 5, 218 / EUD, 219.

of God and therefore sought likeness in ruling. But the resemblance is not like that. . . . The human being and God do not look like each other directly, but inversely; only when God has infinitely become the eternal and omnipresent object of worship and the human being always the worshiper, only then do they look like each other.[39]

To see a human being worship God is to see a reflection of God himself. This is Kierkegaard's reformulation of the ancient doctrine of *analogia entis*,[40] which, among other things, states that human beings—as creatures—stand in a proportional relationship with their creator. They convey the divine being, but this similarity is nonetheless marked by an infinite dissimilarity. One of the outcomes of this teaching is just what we have seen in Kierkegaard's treatment of *Billede*: in the image of Anna, it is possible to indirectly but truly perceive the divine. The aesthetic and the religious are not necessarily opposed.

Kierkegaard and the Dialectic Between the Aesthetic and the Religious

Scholarship on Kierkegaard is known for its diversity. A quick scroll through a bibliography—or even an online bookstore—reveals as much. There are books on Kierkegaard the individualist and on

---

39. SKS 8, 290 / UDVS, 193, my translation.
40. This claim may seem exaggerated, especially in light of Balthasar's evaluation of Kierkegaard's thinking. However, it is worth noting that Balthasar's mentor, the Jesuit philosopher Erich Przywara, expressly linked Kierkegaard to the tradition of *analogia entis* in Catholic thought. See his *Das Geheimnis Kierkegaards* (Munich and Berlin: Verlag von R. Oldenbourg, 1929), 80. Just why Balthasar differed so greatly from Przywara on this question is a mystery in its own right. What is clear is that both thinkers drew on Kierkegaard—typically, Przywara as an ally, Balthasar as a critic—to shed light on Catholicism's status in modernity. For more on this topic, see Joseph Ballan, "Hans Urs von Balthasar: Persuasive Forms or Offensive Signs? Kierkegaard and the Problems of Theological Aesthetics," in *Kierkegaard's Influence on Theology: Tome III: Catholic and Jewish Theology*, ed. Jon Stewart (Farnham: Ashgate Publishing, 2012), 3-24, and Christopher B. Barnett, "Erich Przywara, S.J.: Catholicism's Great Expositor of the 'Mystery' of Kierkegaard,"in *Kierkegaard's Influence on Theology: Tome III: Catholic and Jewish Theology*, ed. Jon Stewart (Farnham: Ashgate Publishing, 2012), 131-51.

Kierkegaard the social commentator, on Kierkegaard the postmodern deconstructionist and on Kierkegaard the guardian of Christian orthodoxy, just to mention a couple of fault lines. And yet, despite this interpretive range, one point seems to have achieved a wide consensus—namely, that Kierkegaard was a master *dialectician*. That, after all, was how Kierkegaard saw himself. In a lengthy 1850 journal passage, after asserting that he is neither a religious zealot nor "only a poet," Kierkegaard underlines the twin pillars of his literary career: "What, then, has helped me in addition to what is of greatest importance, that a Governance has helped me? The fact that I am a dialectician."[41]

With this in mind, it is surprising that a number of commentators have neglected to see this dialectical approach as operative in Kierkegaard's analysis of the aesthetic and the religious. Consider Balthasar once again. He insists that Kierkegaard's thought inexorably leads to a chasm between beauty and faith, between art and religion. This is especially a critique of Kierkegaard's later authorship, with its increasingly strident calls for Christian obedience and suffering. But Balthasar omits examples that run counter to his thesis. There is no mention, say, of Kierkegaard's treatment of Anna, much less a discussion of his nuanced recognition of a "social role for art in the criticism of modern culture."[42] As a result, Kierkegaard's warnings about the misuse of the aesthetic are transformed into categorical rejections of art and of beauty. The dialectical tension is cut, replaced by the resounding thud of Kierkegaard's conception of the religious.

To be sure, as the previous analysis of *Billede* has made clear, Kierkegaard's approach to the aesthetic is hardly so straightforward.

41. SKS 23, NB15:46 / JP 6, 6577.
42. Sylvia Walsh, *Living Poetically: Kierkegaard's Existential Aesthetics* (University Park: Pennsylvania State University Press, 1994), 188.

For one thing, there is little, if any, cause for thinking that Kierkegaard believes the aesthetic can somehow be expunged from human existence. As C. Stephen Evans notes, "[I]t is a universal dimension of human life."[43] The implication here is that Kierkegaard's well-known existential "stages"—the aesthetic, the ethical, and the religious—are not mere steps on a ladder, arranged in such a way that to reach the ethical is to abandon the aesthetic and so on. Rather, these stages are permanent domains within the self, which, like a Venn diagram, overlap one another at certain key junctures. To quote Evans again, "[T]he ethical must in some way be preserved within the religious sphere, even if it is transformed as well, just as the aesthetic must be preserved within the ethical and religious spheres."[44]

This perichoresis of the existential spheres follows from the analysis of the self in Kierkegaard's pseudonymous treatise *The Sickness unto Death*. There, as has been seen, the self is understood as a synthesis of contrary elements—namely, the finite and the infinite, the temporal and the eternal, necessity and freedom. However, the self is not the bare fact that these contrasting elements are in a dialectical relationship; instead, it is the "positive third"[45] that is capable of interacting with its constitutive attributes. In the words of Kierkegaard's pseudonym, Anti-Climacus, the self is "the relation [that] relates itself to itself . . ."[46]

Much could be (and has been) made of this definition. With regard to the present discussion, the decisive point has to do with Anti-Climacus's insistence that the self's goal is not to give priority to one of its features over against the others—for that would be a "misrelation

43. C. Stephen Evans, *Kierkegaard: An Introduction* (Cambridge: Cambridge University Press, 2009), 69.
44. Ibid.
45. SKS 11, 129 / SUD, 13.
46. SKS 11, 129 / SUD, 13.

of despair"[47]—but, rather, to will to be what it is. For example, in his analysis of despair as defined by finitude and infinitude, Anti-Climacus points out that the imaginative faculty is the medium by which persons feel, know, and will. It projects to the self its own possibilities. This is, as far as it goes, good news. But the imagination can become unhinged, leading the self into a kind of "fantasy world," wherein it prefers to associate with potentiality rather than actuality. This is the despair of infinitude. Like Johannes the Seducer, such a self is aroused by abstract images, but cannot bear any *real* contact with the world. At the same time, Anti-Climacus also describes "finitude's despair," which is marked by an inability to imagine possibilities beyond everyday life. Here the self fails to envision its unique potential; it becomes a "number instead of a self . . ."[48] The task, then, is to avoid each of these extremes. The imagination—with its distinctive ability to create and to appreciate images and, in turn, to shape the potential of the self—is an essential component of human life. But it must neither dominate nor retreat. As Anti-Climacus explains, "To become oneself is to become concrete. But to become concrete is neither to become finite nor to become infinite, for that which is to become concrete is indeed a synthesis."[49]

This point sheds light on the status of the aesthetic in Kierkegaard's thought. As a dialectician, he does not posit a stark choice between art and religion, imagination and reality, the infinite and the finite. In other words, the issue is not *whether* the aesthetic has a role in human life and in the development of the self. It is *how* one relates to the aesthetic that is decisive.

This conclusion again calls to mind the earlier discussion of *Billede* in Kierkegaard's authorship. As was noted, Kierkegaard cautions

47. SKS 11, 130 / SUD, 14.
48. SKS 11, 149 / SUD, 33.
49. SKS 11, 146 / SUD, 30.

against the lure of the image, which can draw one out of the real world and into its own ambit. This type of idolatry—a word that, taken from the Greek *eidololatria*, literally means "subservience to an image"—is problematic no matter one's station in life, be it that of a romantic suitor or that of a Christian disciple. On the other hand, Kierkegaard both encourages and exemplifies the use of images as a means of spurring one to existential authenticity. Here the image does not absorb one's attention but, rather, redirects it, providing the observer with an ideal that is met only through concrete appropriation. Indeed, such is the ideal of *faith*, embodied in Kierkegaard's pictures of persons such as Anna, and which Anti-Climacus defines as the very opposite of despair.[50]

Thus Kierkegaard not only leaves the door open for the integration of the aesthetic and the religious but, in fact, makes it a key aspect of his upbuilding literature. For him, the life of faith is beautiful, and its beauty can lead one to God. This is why, as Sylvia Walsh points out, he frequently "declares in the later journals that he is essentially a poet, and in several entries he describes himself more specifically as a 'poet of the religious' and even more narrowly as a 'Christian poet and thinker.'"[51] As such, his role might be compared to any religious artist. For example, the business of the painter or, in traditional terminology, "writer" of Christian icons is neither to issue dogmatic proclamations nor to compose systematic treatises on theology. On the contrary, his artwork is intended to orient the observer toward holiness, to establish contact between the observer and sacred events and lives. The iconographer, then, may draw on the doctrinal tradition—to be sure, it is doctrine, and not the writer per se, that determines the existential ideals—but her goal is fundamentally existential. Likewise, Kierkegaard understood his artistic task as

50. SKS 11, 197 / SUD, 82.
51. Walsh, *Living Poetically*, 224.

creating a "pathos-filled impression of an existential expression of the ideal," so that a "pathos for the existential" is nurtured.[52] An 1850 journal entry puts it in more direct terms:

> Now there will be need for the presentation of the religious in poetic form. This is a step forward compared to what prevails now when meaninglessness and mediocrity actually have taken the place of the religious, so that the poet in the ordinary sense is even higher than the religious.
>
> In any case there no doubt must be something poetic in the religious domain, mainly just to get hold of existential ideals again and to encounter the existential ideals.[53]

This task is implicit in Kierkegaard's *Billeder* of Anna and others. Artistic representation in and of itself is not esteemed but, rather, its service to human flourishing and to God. To cite Walsh once more, "In Kierkegaard's view, the highest existential ideality is to be a Christian. Thus, in his religious writings, he is primarily concerned to portray, like an artist, the ideal picture of a Christian."[54]

The Idol, the Icon, and Kierkegaard

The above discussion has sought to establish two overarching points. First, by examining Kierkegaard's understanding of and approach to the concept of "image," it has shown that Kierkegaard does not posit an ultimate decision between the aesthetic and the religious but, rather, exemplifies their careful integration. Second, it has underlined that Kierkegaard's dialectical approach to this question correlates to the conception of the self developed in *The Sickness unto Death*, not to mention the way in which he viewed his task as an author. What

---

52. SKS 22, NB13:88 / JP 6, 6521.
53. SKS 24, NB21:132 / JP 2, 1792.
54. Walsh, *Living Poetically*, 226.

has emerged is a kind of "aesthetics of the icon"—an aesthetics that points beyond itself, viewing art not as an end in itself but as a means toward religious and, with it, existential fulfillment.

These findings can be illustrated by drawing on the work of the French thinker Jean-Luc Marion, particularly as expounded in his well-known text, *God without Being* [*Dieu sans l'être*]. What follows, then, is by no means a comprehensive reading of Marion's oeuvre, nor is it a suggestion that Kierkegaard's views are somehow identical with Marion's. The idea is more basic—namely, that Marion's reflections can shed light on the various images populating Kierkegaard's works and, in turn, on the Dane's dialectical approach to aesthetic imagery.

Marion's interest in the tension between idol and icon developed over time. In his early work on Descartes, Marion launched an attempt "to disconnect the link between metaphysics and the divine," arguing that metaphysics—to the extent that it defines a supreme being for the sake of understanding other beings—always already lapses into idolatry.[55] In *God without Being*, he "pushes his definition of idolatry further by explicating a distinction between idol and icon."[56] Whereas before he had focused on the "specific idolatry of metaphysics," he now posits a variety of idolatries, "moving from visual to conceptual, from simple to more complex."[57] What these idols have in common is that they satisfy the intentions of those who apprehend them. For example, an image becomes an idol whenever "it suggests to the gaze where to rest."[58] This, in fact, is what makes the idol charming: it relieves the observer of the burden of seeking

55. Christina M. Gschwandtner, *Reading Jean-Luc Marion: Exceeding Metaphysics* (Bloomington: Indiana University Press, 2007), 40–41.
56. Ibid., 43.
57. Ibid., 42–43.
58. Jean-Luc Marion, *God without Being*, trans. Thomas A. Carlson (Chicago: University of Chicago Press, 1991), 12.

something beyond it. As Marion puts it, "The gaze settles only inasmuch as it rests—from the weight of upholding the sight of an aim without term, rest, or end: 'to sleep with the sleep of the earth.'"[59] Idolatry, then, "reveals a sort of essential fatigue,"[60] and this fatigue is perilous. It wants its desires fulfilled on its own terms, and, for that reason, it is closed off to transcendence and, finally, to true divinity. Christina Gschwandtner sums up Marion's point in this way: "[T]he idol does indeed provide a vision of the divine, but a precise vision that is fulfilled in the gaze and thus controlled by it. The observer of the idol grasps hold of the divine."[61]

In contrast, Marion sees the icon as that which "summons the gaze to surpass itself."[62] Indeed, one never really looks *at* the icon, since the icon serves as a medium through which one's vision goes "back . . . up the infinite stream of the invisible."[63] Hence, where the idol offers a circumscribed deity that is effectively a projection of human consciousness, the icon "becomes a kind of window through which the gaze travels toward the 'unenvisageable,' that which cannot ever be contained in a human gaze."[64] This is why Marion refers to the icon as "excessive."[65] It does not so much contain its subject matter as communicate that its subject matter cannot be contained. "Idols abolish distance, while the icon preserves it."[66] With this in mind, Marion points out that, before the icon, it is actually the observer who is being observed: "The icon regards us – it *concerns* us, in that it allows the intention of the invisible to occur visibly."[67] The challenge

---

59. Ibid., 13.
60. Ibid.
61. Gschwandtner, *Marion*, 43.
62. Marion, *God without Being*, 18.
63. Ibid.
64. Gschwandtner, *Marion*, 132. See Marion, *God without Being*, 17.
65. Marion, *God without Being*, 21.
66. Gschwandtner, *Marion*, 132.
67. Marion, *God without Being*, 19. This point recalls Kierkegaard's statement, cited above, that "Christian truth" observes human beings, not the other way around.

facing the iconographer, then, is to allow for this porous quality, to clear the way for the gaze of the invisible while simultaneously acknowledging that the invisible emerges "by its aim"[68] alone. As Marion explains, "The icon lays out the material of wood and paint in such a way that there appears in them the intention of a transpiercing gaze emanating from them."[69] As a result, the "aesthetics of the icon" is, in a certain sense, the absence of aesthetics. For, according to Marion, the idol "supposes an *aesthesis* that precisely imposes its measure on the idol," whereas the icon's "depth withdraws [it] from all aesthetics."[70]

Here—as in all of the above reflections—Marion walks the dialectical tightrope in a way that evokes, or illuminates, Kierkegaard's own approach to aesthetic imagery. Recall that, for Kierkegaard, the danger of the image is that it will close off the observer from reality. This is true of Johannes the Seducer, who would rather fantasize about Cordelia than actually *be* in a relationship with her. But it is also true of religious persons or groups, whenever they reduce the divine to an artistic or conceptual object, as opposed to a living *subject*. It is this circumscribed and attenuated perspective, so deftly portrayed by Kierkegaard, that corresponds to Marion's analysis of idolatry.

And yet, on the other hand, Kierkegaard also uses his pen to paint pictures of holiness. These images of holy persons such as Anna and the woman who was a sinner not only communicate the nature of faith—in particular, how it is a movement of dispossession, whereby the claims of the believer are renounced for the sake of divine adoration—but, in doing so, they echo the divine itself. For Kierkegaard's pictures are indeed "excessive." They convey that what

68. Ibid.
69. Ibid.
70. Ibid., 20.

they convey cannot be conveyed. Far from reducing the divine to human categories, they depict the great distance between human beings and God—a distance that is "closed" only through the paradox of worship, in which the person comes to recognize that he is beheld by the mysterious Other. Here, *in nuce*, is a type of Marion's notion of the icon.

In a well-known remark, the philosopher Martin Heidegger once said of the god of metaphysics: "Before the *causi sui*, man can neither fall to his knees in awe nor can he play music and dance before this god."[71] Kierkegaard would register a similar concern about art and its tendency to reproduce gods of pleasure and utility. But both in practice and theory he suggests it need not be so. When the aesthetic engenders worship, idolatry is supplanted by doxology. This may not be an aesthetics in the classic, Western sense of the term. Rather, it is an aesthetics of the icon.

Conclusion

The conclusion of this chapter is, in a sense, the conclusion of the first three chapters of this study. A good bit of ground has been covered: Kierkegaard has emerged as a figure of interest in Christian spirituality—one who conceived of his authorial mission as "upbuilding," and who developed a corresponding theological anthropology, which treats human fulfillment as an outcome of an ever-deepening relationship with God. Moreover, it has been seen that, despite his famous concerns about the influence of aesthetics on religious practice, he nevertheless insists that Christian faith—the terminus of spiritual development—can be "written" in the form of

71. Martin Heidegger, *Identity and Difference*, trans. Joan Stambaugh (New York: Harper & Row, 1969), 72.

icons. In other words, he does not oppose art and faith but, rather, uses art to *represent* faith.

With these points established, it is now time to turn to the second part of this study, where Kierkegaard's "icons of faith" will be featured. As will be seen in Chapter Four, Kierkegaard views creation itself as bearing iconic significance. And yet, in the end, he places the greatest stress on biblical figures such as John the Baptist, Job, and, of course, Jesus Christ. For Kierkegaard, if we are to know what faith is—and how it relates to spiritual fulfillment—we must contemplate their examples.

4

Icons of Faith:
The Natural World

The Christian tradition has long held that the natural world communicates theological meaning. As the Apostle Paul famously writes, "Ever since the creation of the world [God's] eternal power and divine nature, invisible though they are, have been understood and seen through the things he has made" (Rom. 1:20). Many other Christian thinkers have expanded on Paul's statement. The American Protestant theologian Jonathan Edwards (1703–58) describes the created order as a key part of God's "instruction" of humanity, its majesty "painting . . . forth" spiritual realities that, in turn, harmonize with biblical teaching.[1] Similarly, the English Catholic poet Gerard Manley Hopkins (1844–89) writes that "[t]he world is charged with the grandeur of God,"[2] despite the continuous grind of human life and industry: "[F]or all this [toil], nature is never spent; / There lives the dearest freshness deep down things."[3]

---

1. Jonathan Edwards, "Jonathan Edwards on the Beauty of Creation," in *The Christian Theology Reader*, ed. Alister E. McGrath (Oxford: Blackwell Publishing, 2007), 122–23.
2. Gerard Manley Hopkins, "God's Grandeur," in *God's Grandeur and Other Poems* (Mineola, NY: Dover, 1995), 15.
3. Ibid.

The above views are of varying import, but, at bottom, all share a basic presupposition: Christian faith does not permit a purely "neutral" observation of or interaction with the natural world. To come into contact with nature is to learn something about God and about how human beings are to respond to God. Understood in these terms, creation assumes the kind of iconic quality discussed in the previous chapter. It is so "saturated" with gifts and significance that it points beyond itself to its invisible source.

And yet, if this is true, why is it that Christian thinking often approaches the natural world with reluctance?[4] Part of it, doubtless, has to do with the worry that nature itself can become the object of one's spiritual life. Rather than point to God, it can come to *replace* God. On the other hand, the created order can also be seen as an instrument for human use, a realm of *natura pura* detached from the concerns and aims of the supernatural. This tendency is particularly prominent in a scientific, mechanized society. The grandeur and intricacy of creation can begin to resemble a postcard or a diagram—remarkable but cold. Formally, such a picture might recall a kind of icon, but it lacks the rich textures—the dynamic insights and stories—that underlie and enliven iconography. Icons may appear to be static images, but, in reality, they are "motion pictures," animated by the lives and traditions on which they are founded.

As will be seen, Kierkegaard's pictures of the natural world avoid the above pitfalls. By no means does he forget that "God is in heaven, and [creatures] upon earth" (Eccles. 5:2), nor does he treat nature as a stale entity, interesting solely for the sake of human exploitation. For

---

4. This tendency is more pronounced in certain strands of dogmatic theology than in Christian spirituality: Francis of Assisi (1182–1226) and Thérèse of Lisieux (1873–1897) are just two examples of mystics whose spiritual insights draw frequently from the natural world. Still, even Christian spirituality can be said to exhibit a *tension* between nature and supernature, creation and salvation. But this acknowledgement raises a systematic (and controversial) question that exceeds the scope of the present work.

him, to look upon nature is to look upon a great symbol—an external sign of the human being's internal dynamics, which, when properly narrated, can point the way to faith in God and to human happiness.

The task of this chapter, then, is to trace these "icons of faith" in Kierkegaard's authorship. This will not be an exhaustive exercise, but it should, nevertheless, illuminate and illustrate Kierkegaard's spiritual thought. In Chapter Two, we studied his *theory*, but now we will see that theory fleshed out, sketched, in the figures of trees and ocean, lilies and birds.

Kierkegaard as Natural Scientist?

Kierkegaard was, famously, a "city boy." He lived his entire life in Copenhagen, and only rarely would he venture from the capital city's environs, never making it farther than Berlin. But his reluctance to travel hardly turned him into a homebody. Daily he took walks, flicking at grass and weeds with the tip of his cane as he went and greeting a variety of people along the way. As one of his contemporaries described him: "[T]he thin little man, whom you could meet one moment at Østerport and the next on the entirely opposite side of town, apparently a carefree peripatetic, was recognized by everyone."[5]

For his part, Kierkegaard *needed* to get outside. It was on walks that Kierkegaard, the bachelor, made contact with others. But it was also while walking that he developed himself, both mentally and physically: "I walk my way to health and away from every illness every day. I have walked my way to my best ideas, and I know of no thought so burdensome that one cannot walk away from it."[6]

5. Quoted in Joakim Garff, *Søren Kierkegaard: A Biography*, trans. Bruce H. Kirmmse (Princeton, NJ: Princeton University Press, 2005), 310.
6. Quoted in ibid., 313.

89

That being outside refreshed and stimulated Kierkegaard, then, is without question. What is surprising, however, is that there was a time when Kierkegaard thought of linking his *vocation* to his love of the outdoors and to nature. This interest is discussed in a letter from 1835, penned at a mere twenty-two years of age. Writing to a distant relative—Professor Peter Wilhelm Lund, who pioneered the study of paleontology and zoology in Brazil—Kierkegaard recalls how much he enjoyed hearing "of the impression your first journey into that wondrous nature made upon you . . ."[7] Indeed, as he goes on, Lund's dedication to science has occasioned in him a desire to decide on his own life's work: "I stand like Hercules—not at a crossroads—no, but at a multitude of roads, and therefore it is all the harder to choose the right one."[8] Among these possible "roads" is that of the natural sciences, which Kierkegaard defines quite broadly:

> In this category I include all those who seek to explain and interpret the runic script of nature, ranging from him who calculates the speed of the stars and, so to speak, arrests them in order to study them more closely, to him who describes the physiology of a particular animal, from him who surveys the surface of the earth from the mountain peaks to him who descends to the depths of the abyss. . . .[9]

Though admittedly put off by a certain kind of scientific approach—namely, a single-minded focus on "collecting" and mastering "a great wealth of details"—Kierkegaard nevertheless lauds the "tranquility, the harmony, the joy" that science can bring, if it views "the component parts in their proper light."[10] This is, he says, the method of some of Denmark's greatest scientists, not least Lund

---

7. SKS 17, AA:12 / LD, 42.
8. SKS 17, AA:12 / LD, 43.
9. SKS 17, AA:12 / LD, 44.
10. SKS 17, AA:12 / LD, 44.

himself, and its impact on him has been "salutary."[11] As he sums up, "I have been and am still inspired by the natural sciences . . ."[12]

Joakim Garff has questioned whether or not Lund ever received this letter,[13] but, in any case, it is certain that Kierkegaard evinced a genuine interest in the natural world. Also in 1835, the young student journeyed to northern Zealand—a fairly short jaunt from Copenhagen, even in those days, but still a place where one could take in the beauty of Grib Forest, Lake Esrum, and, of course, the North Sea. Over a period of about two months, he met with an ichthyologist, hiked, collected plants, and watched birds. At one point, after a visit to Gurre Lake, he marveled at the area's pristine beech woodlands, relishing that "'wheel tracks' were now his only 'connection with the world of men.'"[14]

For Garff, there is something comical about this scene. Kierkegaard stands as a "perfect model for a slightly ironic depiction of a Copenhagen intellectual in a natural landscape."[15] But this characterization, while not unfounded, seems to miss the larger point. After all, Kierkegaard himself understood that his relationship with nature went deeper than mere observation. *That*, in fact, was why he rejected the natural sciences as a vocational field: as much as he loved the outdoors, as much as he was drawn to the wood and to the sea, he could never leave behind his fundamental interest in human life and its destiny. This point is also made clear in his letter to Lund. He notes that "life has always interested me most," so much so that "it has always been my desire to clarify and solve the riddle of life."[16] Consequently, nature must be "observed from another side,

---

11. SKS 17, AA:12 / LD, 44.
12. SKS 17, AA:12 / LD, 45.
13. Garff, *Kierkegaard*, 53.
14. Ibid., 55.
15. Ibid., 54.
16. SKS 17, AA:12 / LD, 45.

which does not require insight into the secrets of science."[17] This other "side" is characterized less by *what* he observes than by *how* he observes. It involves an intent to view the natural world as a window into the design and purpose of existence:

> It matters not whether I contemplate the whole world in a single flower or listen to the many hints that nature offers about human life; whether I admire those daring designs on the firmament; or whether, upon hearing the sounds of nature in Ceylon, for example, I am reminded of the sounds of the spiritual world; or whether the departure of the migratory birds reminds me of the more profound yearnings of the human heart.[18]

Nature, then, bespeaks of humanity's relationship with God, and thus it has an importance far beyond the scope of the natural sciences—an importance that Kierkegaard recognized as increasingly forgotten in the modern world. Science, industrialization, and urbanization have given persons a sense of mastery over nature, but, "in a storm, when a hurricane rages and uproots trees . . . [or when] the earth opens up and swallows entire cities,"[19] nature demonstrates that it is subservient to God alone. And therein lies a final reason to contemplate the natural world: to do so serves as a check against human hubris and insularity. As Kierkegaard explains, "Really, we need to live more with nature if for no other reason than to get more of an impression of God's majesty. Huddled together in the great cultural centers we have as much as possible abolished all overwhelming impressions—a lamentable demoralization."[20]

This comment clarifies why Kierkegaard chose to spend so much time outdoors, whether on walks through the boulevards and parks of Copenhagen or on excursions to the forest and to the seaside. He was

17. SKS 17, AA:12 / LD, 45.
18. SKS 17, AA:12 / LD, 45.
19. SKS 24, NB25:59 / JP 3, 2853.
20. SKS 24, NB25:59 / JP 3, 2853.

seeking *upbuilding*—a point that also discloses why he turned away from a career as a natural scientist and opted for an authorial vocation instead. He did not want to extract bare information from the natural world, but, rather, to see it as a window, an *icon*, of the human spirit and its quest to return to God. It is in this same vein that one should regard the icons of nature in his authorship.

Praising Autumn—and Recollection

When Kierkegaard died on the evening of November 11, 1855, he left behind a prodigious authorship . . . and just a percentage of it published. Indeed, as Kierkegaard's nephew, Henrik Sigvard Lund, sifted through and organized the remnants of his uncle's literary career, he found "cases and boxes and sacks and chests of drawers, in which rolled-up manuscripts and portfolios and notebooks and letters and bills and loose strips and scraps of paper lay . . ."[21] It was a daunting prospect, so much so that Lund put the materials in storage. There they remained for a few years, until they were sent to Kierkegaard's older brother, Peter Christian, who promptly stored them away himself. It was not until 1865—a full decade after Kierkegaard's death, his documents now "covered with a *thick* layer of mould"[22]—that their recovery began in earnest.

Among these loose papers, tucked away in a cabinet in Kierkegaard's basement, was a draft of a larger work on Kierkegaard's favorite season—autumn. He had, it seems, first conceived of the project in 1845, when he dashed off a brief journal entry entitled, "Discourse of Praise for Autumn" [*Lovetale over Efteraaret*]. In it he describes autumn as a time of change and contrast, when cool winds

21. Garff, *Kierkegaard*, 805.
22. Quoted in ibid., 806.

clash with summer heat and the forest "changes color even as one is looking at it."[23] It is as if everything is moving—the wind, the leaves, the temperature, the clouds. In this way, he notes, autumn signifies "the transience of life" and thus "brings out yearning."[24] This desire is deep and even instinctive: just as a woman arouses a man by putting on colorful clothes, so do the changes of autumn call out to the observer, "[H]urry, hurry!"[25]

But to what, exactly, do the changing conditions of autumn hurry us? These are the sorts of questions that Kierkegaard planned to address when he returned to the theme a year or so later. A series of journal entries—headed, again, by the title, "Discourse of Praise for Autumn"—indicate that he intended to write a five-part encomium to autumn, with the first four discourses representing a particular facet of the season and a final one "ending with a *tutti*,"[26] a union of the previous elements. Presumably, the finished product was to function like his upbuilding discourses: by focusing on some aspect of earthly life, he sought to stir—or, in his words, "to mystify"[27]—the reader and thereby to prompt inward deepening. For him, then, to attend to autumn is to engage in a kind of mystical activity, propelling one into the secrets of existence.

The first part of the eulogy is not clearly marked, nor developed in any detail, but it appears to have been a general ode to the season, proclaiming "Long live autumn!" and "[A]utumn alone is *the season*."[28] The next entry, however, is designated "No. 2," and it sets about a specific theme—namely, "*Autumn is the Time of the* **Clouds**."[29] According to Kierkegaard, the clouds of autumn are hurried and ever

23. SKS 18, JJ:367 / JP 3, 2833, my translation.
24. SKS 18, JJ:367 / JP 3, 2833, my translation.
25. SKS 18, JJ:367 / JP 3, 2833.
26. SKS 27, P344:1 / JP, 2842.
27. SKS 27, P341 / JP 3, 2840.
28. SKS 27, P342–343 / JP 3, 2840–41.

changing: they move along "like vagabond dreams," evolving from shape to shape and colliding with one another "in jolly games."[30] This movement stands in contrast to summertime, when "they are too indolent and sleepy."[31] One might nap of a summer's day, but in autumn one walks, quickly, with the wind and clouds.

It is in this sense of motion that, for Kierkegaard, autumn's clouds resemble thinking. He draws on Norse mythology to flesh out this point: according to legend, the universe was fashioned from the remains of the slain giant Ymer, whose brains became the clouds. "And truly there is no better symbol for clouds than thoughts and no better symbol for thought than clouds—clouds are brain-weaving, and what else are thoughts."[32] Thus he connects autumn and its briskness with a peculiar sort of thinking: "Stand still, you who call yourself a thinker, and watch the clouds—during autumn. If you have ever thought about it before, think about it again."[33] What Kierkegaard is recommending is *reflection*—literally, thought bending back on itself. The clouds of autumn have become an image of the human being's unique capacity to wonder, to imagine, to recall, and to do so again. As will be discussed below, this was a theme to which Kierkegaard intended to return in more detail.

The discourse's third part, *"Autumn is the Time of* **Sounds**,*"* is hastily drawn. In effect, it reiterates the preceding theme of movement. As Kierkegaard puts it elsewhere, "[S]ound is motion made audible."[34]

---

29. SKS 27, P341:1 / JP 3, 2842. The entry is written in the first person, though, if finished, Kierkegaard would have almost certainly attributed it to a pseudonym, based on his note that the five discourses would be assigned to "5 persons" (Ibid.).
30. SKS 27, P341:1 / JP 3, 2842.
31. SKS 27, P341:1 / JP 3, 2842.
32. SKS 27, P341:1 / JP 3, 2842.
33. SKS 27, P341:1 / JP 3, 2842.
34. SKS 27, P344:3 / JP 3, 2844.

The fourth part is more substantively outlined. Entitled "*Autumn is the Time* of **Colors**," it is, intriguingly, the darkest of the proposed treatises. Kierkegaard begins by pointing out that color signifies the presence of "unrest."[35] With this term he is underlining the connection between color and change. Eternal forms such as triangles have no need of color, since they are beyond time and alteration. Likewise, "the unremittingly blue heaven is certainly not color," for "[c]olor is contrast, but contrast is unrest, motion . . . ."[36] With this in mind, Kierkegaard makes the connection to autumn: "In contrast to summer, we may say that the distinguishing feature of autumn is that it changes colors. . . . [T]he contrasts during autumn are so intensely in motion every moment that it is like a constant shifting."[37] Of course, autumn's changes have to do with the transition from summer to winter. It is a time of slow but certain decline, as the green hues of summer fade to earthy maizes and maroons and, finally, disappear altogether. Hence, as Kierkegaard notes, autumn is often associated with melancholy, though he does not think this an altogether just comparison. For autumn's specter of death recollects summer's "desire" for life; the relentless coming of decay brings the beauty of existence into relief.[38] This insight dovetails into one of Kierkegaard's most striking pictures:

> Look—at your feet the straw withers; if you will look very carefully, you will see that every straw has its own color. Meanwhile, the beech tree holds itself erect. It will not bow; it will not yield; it wistfully shakes its head, but then it proudly shakes off the withered leaves again; it would rather have a few leaves which are not withered than all those withered ones. How curious it is that in the summer time no one really sees that a green leaf is really green, no one sees the poetry in the green of summer. . . . But in the autumn! When the birch tree stands bare, with only one

35. SKS 27, P344:3 / JP 3, 2844, my translation.
36. SKS 27, P344:3 / JP 3, 2844, my translation.
37. SKS 27, P344:3 / JP 3, 2844.
38. SKS 27, P344:3 / JP 3, 2844, my translation.

single green but freshly green leaf on its naked branch, then you see the color *green*, you see it by contrast.[39]

What autumn represents, then, is a "battle for life," and in this effort it is "heroic."[40]

The fifth and would-be final piece of the "Discourse of Praise for Autumn" is called "*Autumn Is the Time of* **Recollections**." Kierkegaard does not delineate it with much detail, though he leaves clues as to its purpose, namely, to conclude on a note of hope. After experimenting with an analogy between memory and cooking—which lauds memory's capacity to change the odious into the satisfying, just as a great chef can "make a delicacy out of even the most unpalatable ingredients"—he rejects it for lacking proper "pathos."[41] In other words, such a playful metaphor fails to do justice to the earnestness of the present essay. "[T]his discourse should be delivered in the purest and noblest spirit, in order to create a contrast to the despair in the others,"[42] as Kierkegaard explains.

This is an important remark, which sheds light on how the "Discourse of Praise for Autumn," even in its partial state, functions as a spiritual icon. First, Kierkegaard here demarcates between the despair of the preceding treatises—which largely concern *change*—and the hopefulness of the present treatise on *recollection*. In this distinction between change and recollection lies a key aspect of Kierkegaardian spirituality. As discussed in Chapter Two, Kierkegaard views the human being as suspended, so to speak, between the flux of time and the rest of eternity. The beauty of the former often belies its pain, for the person wed to time is, ultimately, wed to death. Thus Kierkegaard enjoins his reader to detach,

---

39. SKS 27, P344:3 / JP 3, 2844, my translation.
40. SKS 27, P344:3 / JP 3, 2844.
41. SKS 27, P344:4 / JP 3, 2845.
42. SKS 27, P344:4 / JP 3, 2845.

however painfully, from the allurements of the temporal order and to become grounded in the eternal through faith. In Kierkegaard's theological anthropology, this is not an abandonment of time but, rather, its proper fulfillment. After all, the self is neither temporal nor eternal; it is a *synthesis* of the two.

For Kierkegaard, recollection is an aid to this process of detachment—a point that hints at why autumn, the season of recollection, so appealed to him. To picture the changes of autumn, with its shifting winds and changing colors, is to picture its temporality and, indeed, the temporality of all earthly life, including the self. Thus it brings the human being's fundamental situation to light. Just as the death of winter looms over the beauty of autumn, so does a twofold death loom over the beauty of human existence. There is, of course, biological death, and yet there is something worse: *the sickness unto death*. As Anti-Climacus writes, "Christianly understood . . . not even death is 'the sickness unto death'; even less so is everything that goes under the name of earthly and temporal suffering . . ."[43] This sickness unto death—the worst of all deaths—is despair/sin. It is responsible for sundering the human being from her divine source and, indeed, from life itself. The unrest of autumn recalls this change of state: the fall (to use the colloquial term for the season) is a type of the other Fall. In both cases, life has not been snuffed out altogether, but time is short and winter nigh.

This sense of unrest and disorder is preserved in Kierkegaard's concept of *religious* recollection. That, in point of fact, is what distinguishes it from other sorts of recollection, which seek to take flight into the eternal. The aesthetic-minded person, for instance, seeks to perpetuate pleasure by bringing it back into consciousness:

43. SKS 11, 124 / SUD, 8.

[The aesthete] consciously "photographs" into one's memory the high spots of special pleasure-giving events as they happen. Then later, at one's leisure, one can recall the event and thus reexperience the pleasure. In this way one "eternalizes" it in one's memory. The experience of recollection is thus different from remembering an event as it happened. . . .[44]

Thus aesthetic recollection must be refused: it constitutes a break from reality, since past is past and cannot be "re-called" *in toto*. Another incomplete, if more appealing, form of recollection comes from Plato, who advocates for a recollection of eternal truth—which is latent in the human soul—over against the imperfect world of sense experience. Here, at least, that which is truly eternal is sought, but sacrificed in the process is present human experience and, with it, the concrete, time-bound aspect of the human self.

For Kierkegaard, then, a properly religious recollection will not seek the eternal at the expense of "future-orientated, ongoing existence."[45] To return to the imagery of autumn, it will not ignore the season's changing winds and disturbing colors but, rather, contemplate *with* them. Despair and sin, including the ineluctable "winter" of death, must be confronted and incorporated into the self's unfolding quest for eternity. And yet, this recollection of sin makes clear that the self as such is not eternal and thus eternality must be found elsewhere—namely, in God through faith. As Johannes Climacus explains, "[W]hen the retreat out of existence into eternity by way of recollection has been made impossible, then, with the truth facing one as the paradox, in the anxiety of sin and its pain . . . there is no stronger expression for inwardness than—to have faith."[46] Faith, then, is not brought into relief by the comfort of summer but

44. Julia Watkin, *Historical Dictionary of Kierkegaard's Philosophy* (Lanham, MD: Scarecrow, 2001), 208.
45. Ibid., 209.
46. SKS 7, 193 / CUP1, 209–10.

by the disquiet of autumn. "In the religious sphere, the positive is distinguished by the negative; the relation to an eternal happiness is distinguished by suffering,"[47] as Climacus puts it.

Though unfinished, Kierkegaard's "Discourse of Praise for Autumn" nicely reflects this point. Kierkegaard invites the reader to let the images of westerly winds and October trees point the way to the rest found only in God. The season of autumn—"When yellow leaves, or none, or few, do hang / Upon those boughs which shake against the cold"[48]—has become an icon of faith.

The Lilies of the Field and the Birds of the Air

Despite its range and size, Kierkegaard's oeuvre exhibits a number of patterns. There is, of course, his peculiar ascription of authorship to either pseudonyms or to himself, not to mention a cache of philosophical and theological concepts—"irony," "paradox," and "repetition," just to name a few—that turn up throughout his writings. Furthermore, certain persons, quotations, and stories appear regularly: we see Socrates as early as 1838's *From the Papers of One Still Living* and as late as 1855's *The Changelessness of God*. James 1:17-22, perhaps Kierkegaard's most cherished biblical passage, is invoked in writings from 1843, 1848, 1851, and 1855. What these recurring patterns suggest is that Kierkegaard's intensity was as impressive as his extensity. Like a miner, he repeatedly burrowed into the ideas and the figures from which he drew intellectual and spiritual sustenance.

This is also the case with another one of Kierkegaard's "icons of faith"—the lilies of the field and the birds of the air. Not only

---

47. SKS 7, 484 / CUP1, 532.

48. William Shakespeare, "Sonnet 73," in *Shakespeare's Sonnets: With Detailed Notes from the World's Leading Center of Shakespeare Studies*, eds. Barbara A. Mowat and Paul Werstine (New York: Washington Square Press, 2004), 151.

are there scores of references to "lilies" and to "birds" throughout Kierkegaard's corpus—far too many, in fact, to catalog here—but he wrote three proper treatises on the subject. The first is called "What We Learn from the Lilies in the Field and from the Birds of the Air: Three Discourses," and it comprises the second part of 1847's *Upbuilding Discourses in Various Spirits*. The second treatise, "The Cares of the Pagans: Christian Discourses,"[49] also belongs to a larger work, namely, 1848's *Christian Discourses*. And, finally, there is *The Lily in the Field and the Bird of the Air*, which Kierkegaard issued as a "little book"[50] in 1849. It is clear, then, that Kierkegaard was interested in the subject. But why? What do flowers and birds have to do with the spiritual life?

The immediate impetus behind Kierkegaard's treatment of the lilies of the field and the birds of the air is Matt. 6:24-34—one of the more famous passages in Jesus' Sermon on the Mount:

> No one can serve two masters; for a slave will either hate the one and love the other, or be devoted to the one and despise the other. You cannot serve God and wealth.

> Therefore I tell you, do not worry about your life, what you will eat or what you will drink, or about your body, what you will wear. Is not life more than food, and the body more than clothing? Look at the birds of the air; they neither sow nor reap nor gather into barns, and yet your heavenly Father feeds them. Are you not of more value than they? And can any of you by worrying add a single hour to your span of life? And why do you worry about clothing? Consider the lilies of the field, how they grow; they neither toil nor spin, yet I tell you, even Solomon in all his glory was not clothed like one of these. But if God so clothes the grass of the field, which is alive today and tomorrow is thrown into the oven, will he not much more clothe you—you of little faith? Therefore do not worry, saying, "What will we eat?" or "What will we drink?" or

---

49. This essay is an extended meditation on "the lilies and the birds," though the title itself does not indicate it.
50. SKS 11, 9 / WA, 3.

"What will we wear?" For it is the Gentiles who strive for these things; and indeed your heavenly Father knows that you need all these things. But strive first for the kingdom of God and his righteousness, and all these things will be given to you as well.

So do not worry about tomorrow, for tomorrow will bring worries of its own. Today's trouble is enough for today.

According to M. Eugene Boring, Jesus directs these words to his disciples—as opposed to the "general public"—and they "represent a radical call to decide to move away from cultural values into a life of trust and obedience."[51] But with this call also comes encouragement, which is articulated in Jesus' appeal to nature. As Boring writes, "[P]eople are not called to become birds or lilies, but to consider God's providence for all creation, including birds, lilies, and human beings."[52] The "faith" of the natural world images the healing faith of Christianity.

Kierkegaard's treatises on the lilies and the birds effectively build on this point, albeit in various ways. Just as one can look at, say, Andrei Rublev's icon of the Trinity and discern a variety of meanings, so do Kierkegaard's pictures of the lilies and the birds offer multiple views on God, humanity, and the reconciling promise of faith. This point will be demonstrated below, with particular reference to Kierkegaard's earliest and most comprehensive treatment of the subject—namely, his discourses from 1847.

51. M. Eugene Boring, "The Gospel of Matthew: Introduction, Commentary, and Reflections," in *The New Interpreter's Bible: A Commentary in Twelve Volumes* (Nashville: Abingdon, 1995), 8:214.
52. Ibid., 211.

Learning How to *Be* Human

Throughout its long history, Christian theology has struggled to balance appreciation for creation with recognition that, on the wrong side of the Fall, the world is a deeply flawed, even sinful place. This tension manifested itself in the early church's rejection of Gnosticism, a multifaceted religious movement that, among other things, understood salvation as deliverance from the *body*. Hence, in the gnostic schema, human existence is a lamentable condition, since the human spirit is bound up with corrupted matter. The secret of happiness is to leave this condition behind.

The discussion of Kierkegaard's anthropology in Chapter Two has already disclosed why he would not fall into the gnostic camp. Not only does he preserve the classic Christian understanding of human nature as a spiritual-somatic synthesis, but he insists that despair arises precisely when this union is, as it were, thrown off-kilter. For him, the spirit should not receive priority over the body, nor vice versa. Both elements are essential to human being and, in turn, to human flourishing.

That Kierkegaard, then, composed a treatise on the greatness of being human should not be surprising.[53] His vehicle for doing so is another matter. For it is in "What We Learn from the Lilies in the Field and from the Birds of the Air"—a treatise about the natural world—that he turns to the theme of the good of human life.

Kierkegaard makes clear from the start that the lilies and the birds are "teachers," but not of the usual sort. While human teachers

---

53. Even with Kierkegaard's acerbic attack on the Danish state church at his life's end—an attack that, at its harshest, evokes a gnostic depreciation of material reality—he never renounced the theological anthropology of *The Sickness unto Death*. One might argue, then, that Kierkegaard failed to live up to the principles of Anti-Climacus, but not that he denied them. In this failure, however, he is revealed to be what he always claimed to be—a flawed human being, whose insight into Christianity, however penetrating, ought not be confused with its perfect performance.

instruct with words and confront their interlocutors, the lilies and the birds are silent. Persons look at them, but they direct their gaze elsewhere. In this way, they are like icons, and, indeed, it is more than a little significant that Kierkegaard uses the traditional language of contemplative practice in describing them:

> [O]ut where the lily blooms so beautifully, in the field, up there where the bird is freely at home, in the heavens, if comfort is being sought—there is unbroken silence; no one is present there, and everything is sheer persuasion.

> Yet this is so only if the person . . . actually gives his *attention* to the lilies and the birds and their life and forgets himself in *contemplation* of them and their life, while in his *absorption* in them he, unnoticed, by himself learns something about himself—unnoticed, since there is indeed sheer silence, no one present. The . . . person is free of any and all co-knowledge, except God's, his own—and the lilies'.[54]

This call to contemplation, Kierkegaard adds, is implicit in Jesus' own words: "*Look at the lilies in the field,*" look at them—that is, pay close attention to them, make them the object—not of a fleeting glimpse in passing but of your contemplation [*Betragtning*]."[55] Thus Kierkegaard suggests that his discourse is a contemplative aid: it is tendered for "properly looking at"[56] the lilies and the birds.

But what does one learn from this practice? In other words, what does Kierkegaard want his discourse, his icon, to show? First, he contends that to consider the lilies in the field is to find contentment in one's humanity. This discovery has to do with the lilies's quiet confidence in God—a confidence that is manifested in a variety of ways. As he points out, these lilies are not just any lilies but "the lilies in the field" and thus, in worldly terms, "abandoned lilies."[57] No

---

54. SKS 8, 261 / UDVS, 161–62, my emphasis.
55. SKS 8, 262 / UDVS, 162, my translation.
56. SKS 8, 261 / UDVS, 162.
57. SKS 8, 262 / UDVS, 163.

gardener tends to them, nor are they valued by the wealthy. Bereft of human care, it would seem, then, that they must work to survive. But Kierkegaard, following the words of Jesus, says otherwise: "No, *they do not work*; it is only the rare flowers that require so much work to get them to grow."[58] Here Kierkegaard alludes to one of the key points of his discourse: the lilies do not flourish through activity but through *passivity*. They do not fashion their beauty; it is received from God. As he writes, "[The lily] does not work, it does not spin—it only adorns itself or, more correctly, it is adorned."[59]

That the lily *is* beautiful, Kierkegaard adds, is evident if one will only overlook its commonness and take time to ponder it. Here his mutual appreciation for natural science and contemplation again manifests itself. He argues that the more human beings know about even the humblest of creatures, the more the intricacy and wonder of creation is revealed: "[B]y means of the magnifying glass no one has ever discovered that the lily became less lovely, less ingenious; on the contrary, it proved the lily to be more and more lovely, more and more ingenious."[60] Yet, if this is true, then how much more true is it of that almost impossibly complex and nuanced creature—the human being. As Kierkegaard puts it, "[E]xactly in the same sense, [the human being], without working, without spinning, without any meritoriousness, is more glorious than Solomon's glory by being a human being."[61] Just by virtue of existing, regardless of any individual qualities or achievements, each human being is magnificent, wonderful.

Ordinarily, however, people fail to perceive the fundamental good of being human. They either are too busy to really think about it, or they are too worried about comparing themselves with others.

58. SKS 8, 263 / UDVS, 163.
59. SKS 8, 263 / UDVS, 163.
60. SKS 8, 264 / UDVS, 164.
61. SKS 8, 265 / UDVS, 165.

Kierkegaard illustrates this point—in the manner of a children's story—with his parable of the "worried lily." The lily, he begins, had once been happy, resting beside a little brook, the time happily passing "like the running water that murmurs and disappears."[62] But one day the lily was visited by a bird. The bird had traveled far and wide and regaled the lily with tales about more beautiful places and more beautiful lilies. The bird's talk upset the lily. Suddenly it felt inadequate and grew disenchanted with its surroundings. The brook was no longer soothing but monotonous; the nearby nettles now seemed like inferior companions. Thus the lily asked the bird to take it elsewhere, and "with its beak [the bird] pecked the soil away from the root of the lily so that it could become free."[63] The bird took the lily under its wing with the intention of taking it somewhere better, but, alas, the lily withered on the way. As Kierkegaard sums up, "If the worried lily had been contented with being a lily, it would not have become worried; if it had not become worried, it would have remained standing where it stood—where it stood in all its loveliness . . ."[64]

Here the lily's death reflects the *spiritual* death that, according to Kierkegaard, comes through comparison. The Danish word for "comparison" is *Sammenligning*, and it literally means "joint assessment." To compare, then, is to judge the worth of one thing in relation to another similar thing. Kierkegaard does not dispute that comparison has its uses. Nor does he deny that worry can arise outside of comparison—say, when one is hungry or thirsty. Nevertheless, for him, trouble arises when one human being compares himself with another, for this act puts "the human being in someone else's place or [puts] someone else in his place."[65] In this

---

62. SKS 8, 266 / UDVS, 167.
63. SKS 8, 268 / UDVS, 168.
64. SKS 8, 169 / UDVS, 169.
65. SKS 8, 268–69 / UDVS, 169.

way, comparison violates one of the central tenets of *The Sickness unto Death*, namely, that human happiness entails a self-conscious willingness to be what one is. In contrast, the person comparing is more interested in what she is not.

Kierkegaard relates this spiritual problem to the practical concern of earning a living. With the help of another parable—this one about a worried bird—he distinguishes between the dignity of work and the deceit of self-sustenance. The former is characterized by conscious cooperation with God: the human being works, but always with the recognition that "the heavenly Father feeds him."[66] The latter arises when the person "thinks he supports himself by his labors."[67] Not only is this view false, notes Kierkegaard, but it brings anxiety with it. The person is no longer content with being a human, but is now consumed with "worry about making a living."[68] This concern is present even if one is wealthy, for, as Kierkegaard points out, the issue is not *what* one has but *how* one relates to it. Whether the person is trying to rise in economic status or is already on top, he has worry just to the extent that an "imagined need" (to fall into this or that class, to attain a degree of financial security beyond today) has come to replace "actual need" (food, drink, shelter).[69] This spiritual imbalance results, once again, from comparison. Indeed, the very distinction between "rich" and "poor" fosters the anxiety of comparison: it drives one to focus more on what one lacks than on what one has. But this is, quite literally, a "dis-ease." It unsettles the self by fixing its attention on earthly distinctions rather than on its irreducible worth.

Kierkegaard concludes with an ironic observation. Much of human comparison emerges from a desire to be free. The person concerned with beauty desires the self-reliance that comes with being attractive,

66. SKS 8, 276 / UDVS, 177.
67. SKS 8, 276 / UDVS, 177.
68. SKS 8, 276 / UDVS, 177.
69. SKS 8, 277 / UDVS, 179.

since, presumably, the beautiful person is able to have her pick of suitors. Likewise, the person concerned with wealth desires the self-sufficiency that seems to follow from having an abundance of money at hand. Yet, says Kierkegaard, such independence is unreal: it is bound up with human distinctions that, in the end, are merely accidental. Only that which is essential—the simple good of being human, created by God—can nurture true freedom.

Thus the adage "free as a bird" discloses a powerful truth, for the bird's freedom consists in its contentment to live from divine providence. "To be dependent on one's treasure—that is dependence and hard and heavy slavery; to be dependent on God, completely dependent—that is independence."[70] As Kierkegaard adds, this insight is not his own. It is not a product of human genius. Rather, it is given through the contemplation of the "divinely appointed teachers: the lilies in the field and the birds of the air."[71]

The *Glory* of Being Human

The preceding discussion has underlined that, for Kierkegaard, the contemplation of the lilies and the birds has the capacity for spiritual healing. Caught up in the competing interests of quotidian life—and the frantic comparison that accompanies it—the person can all too easily fall into despair. But the lilies and the birds point in a different direction. If one will detach from everyday worries and take time to consider these natural "icons," a window to a happier, more complete life will open. Here the unfathomable, all-encompassing immutability of the eternal manifests itself beyond the chaotic difference of earthly existence.

70. SKS 8, 279 / UDVS, 181.
71. SKS 8, 280 / UDVS, 182.

Kierkegaard returns to this theme as he begins the second discourse of "What We Learn from the Lilies in the Field and from the Birds of the Air," namely, "How Glorious It Is to Be a Human Being." In a way that strikingly anticipates the thought of Jean-Luc Marion—a similarity already examined in Chapter Three—Kierkegaard distinguishes between *staring* at the lilies and the birds and *surrendering* to them. To stare, in effect, is to remain locked within the confines of one's own cares. "When the eyes are staring, they are looking fixedly ahead, are continually looking at one thing, and yet they are not actually seeing, because, as science explains, the eyes see their own seeing."[72] In contrast, to see aright is to let one's eyes move, to give oneself over to that which presents itself to vision. Kierkegaard calls this form of seeing a "godly diversion."[73]

Unlike various forms of entertainment, a godly diversion does not intend to make the time *seem* to go faster. Such an attempt is spurious, for human beings have no control over time. But it is also counterproductive, since it has the effect of making the time *after* the amusement seem longer. The result, as is plain in contemporary society, is the desire for more and more entertainment.

A godly diversion, however, "diverts, calms, and persuades the more devoutly one gives oneself over to it."[74] This is because it does not seek to pass the time but, rather, to ground it. As Kierkegaard explains,

How different it is with the godly diversion! Have you ever looked at the starlit sky, and have you ever really found a more dependable sight! It costs nothing, and so there is no incitement of impatience; nothing is said about this evening, even less about ten o'clock sharp. Oh no, it waits for you, although in another sense it does not wait for you—the stars now twinkling in the night have done so, unchanged, for centuries.[75]

72. SKS 8, 282 / UDVS, 184.
73. SKS 8, 282 / UDVS, 184.
74. SKS 8, 282 / UDVS, 184.

So, while entertainment emerges from and returns one to boredom, a godly diversion emerges from and returns one to eternity. Thus a godly diversion lacks the loud yet hollow noise of entertainment. One must pause and submit to it, but "when that [submission] is made, then the stillness of diversion grows, and in that stillness grows the persuasion."[76] For if entertainment attracts with the "barker's voice" and the "cannon's thunder," eternity draws one in with its unassuming regularity.[77]

Such is the case with the lilies and the birds, and—using his discourse as an occasion for godly diversion—Kierkegaard revisits their significance. He begins by commenting on how God "clothes" created things such as the lily:

> The beautifully shaped spathe of the stalk, the delicate lines of the leaves, the lovely shades and blends of colors, the whole opulence, if I may put it this way, of ribbons and bows and finery—all this belongs to the lily's clothing, and it is God who clothes it this way. "Would he not much more clothe you, you of little faith?"[78]

These last words are meant to provide comfort, Kierkegaard notes. They underline "not only that the human being is clothed as the grass is clothed but that he is clothed far more gloriously."[79] In other words, by virtue of the "ingenious creation of the human body,"[80] the human being ought to revel in his God-given splendor. Just *being* human is glorious.

Why, then, does it rarely feel that way? The culprit, once again, is comparison, which divides one's thoughts and, in turn, keeps one from attaining the "noble rest of simple thoughts."[81] The use of the

75. SKS 8, 283 / UDVS, 185.
76. SKS 8, 283 / UDVS, 186.
77. SKS 8, 283 / UDVS, 186.
78. SKS 8, 285 / UDVS, 187.
79. SKS 8, 285 / UDVS, 188.
80. SKS 8, 288 / UDVS, 190.
81. SKS 8, 286 / UDVS, 188, my translation.

word "rest" [Ro] here is significant, for it looks forward to Anti-Climacus's understanding of faith as a "transparent rest" in God. In both cases, Ro entails detachment from a twofold unreality—that of fantasy on one hand and of materialism on the other. In contrast, comparison serves to conjure up each of these spiritual demons. It preoccupies persons with categories and distinctions that are accidental, ephemeral, and ultimately artificial—after all, in a state of nature, there are no advanced degrees, tax brackets, or political offices—even as it tempts persons to sheer worldliness, trapping them like "miners" in the "low underground regions of comparisons."[82] Eventually these miners will fail to perceive the wonder of creation and instead gauge their worth solely by what they possess: they, like Gollum in J. R. R. Tolkien's *The Lord of the Rings*, will turn into "beasts."[83]

If comparison, then, imprisons the spiritual life, the godly diversion of contemplating the lilies and the birds frees it—indeed, by breaking the spell of human comparison. The lilies and the birds, in other words, remind the contemplative of her singular role in the cosmos, of the fact that only human beings bear the image of God and only human beings are capable of relating to God. This relationship is perfected in worship:

> To be spirit, that is the human being's invisible glory. Thus when the worried one out in the field stands surrounded by all the witnesses, when every single flower says to him, "Remember God!" he replies, "I will indeed do that, my children—I will worship him, and you poor little ones cannot do that." Consequently the erect, upright one is a worshiper. The upright gait is the sign of distinction, but to be able to prostrate oneself in adoration and worship is even more glorious; and all nature is like the great staff of servants who remind the human being, the ruler, about worshiping God. . . . It is glorious to be clothed as

82. SKS 8, 287 / UDVS, 189.
83. SKS 8, 288 / UDVS, 190.

the lily, even more glorious to be the erect and upright ruler, but most glorious to be nothing by worshiping![84]

This insight, Kierkegaard adds, is a unique contribution of the Christian tradition.[85] Paganism seeks to reproduce divine power and so forgets God. "[T]he resemblance is not like that—no, then instead it is taken in vain."[86] Christianity, properly understood, reveals God as the one who underlies all existence and, therefore, as one who cannot be imitated in the strict sense of the term. Rather, the only way to relate to God is to comply *with* him, to find repose *in* him. This is worship. As Kierkegaard explains, "To worship is not to rule, and yet worship is what makes the human being resemble God, and to be able to worship is the excellence of the invisible glory above all creation."[87] In *The Sickness unto Death*, Anti-Climacus will describe this movement as faith.

In conclusion, Kierkegaard notes that, once humanity's special place in creation has been understood, the *spiritual* burden of earthly life is lifted. Something like work, so often experienced as drudgery and tribulation, looks quite different when viewed as cooperation with God. Here again nature provides the relevant contrast. "The bird does not work," for in its innocence it "gets its food just as a tramp gets his subsistence out in the country."[88] But the glory of the human being is that he "is working together with God—that is, he is God's co-worker."[89]

Whether in faith or in work, then, the glory of human life is that it is a conscious participation in the life of God. This truth,

---

84. SKS 8, 290 / UDVS, 193.
85. Given Kierkegaard's own context and interests, it makes sense to simply say "Christian tradition," though one might invoke other faith traditions here as well.
86. SKS 8, 290 / UDVS, 193.
87. SKS 8, 290 / UDVS, 193.
88. SKS 8, 295 / UDVS, 198–99.
89. SKS 8, 295 / UDVS, 199.

says Kierkegaard, is all too easy to overlook amid day-to-day concerns—thus the importance of the "icon" of the lilies and the birds. In contemplation, the person is reminded of the meaning of human existence, "if he will just look at the bird."[90]

The Promise of Being Human

Icons are hardly monolithic. For every serene depiction of Madonna and Child there are just as many of Christ nailed to the cross. Moreover, even similar pictures can carry different connotations. An icon of the crucified Christ from the patristic era can appear almost tranquil in comparison with the gruesome yet captivating Isenheim Altarpiece of Matthias Grünewald (c.1470–1528). If, following Marion, icons point beyond themselves to what is real, they do so in such a way that reality is revealed to be excessive, bursting with meaning.

As Kierkegaard begins the third and final section of "What We Learn from the Lilies in the Field and from the Birds of the Air," he illustrates this point. The beauty of the lilies and the birds, which reminds the person of his divine origin and intrinsic goodness, also gestures to darker aspects of earthly life—in particular, the ominous specter of death and the related threat of anonymity. Jesus himself calls to mind these dangers. He mentions that, though alive today, the grass will be cast into the fire tomorrow. Likewise, despite their elegance, birds are caught and "sold for a penny." Kierkegaard expands on this notion with pathos:

> Alas, one sparrow has no value at all—there must be two if the buyer is to give one penny. What a change: so joyful, so happy—and now not worth a penny. This is how the bird dies. How hard to die this way! When the first swallow returns in the spring, we all greet it joyfully, but

90. SKS 8, 296 / UDVS, 200.

whether it was the same one that was here last year, well, no one knows that; no one knows it, and therefore no one can recognize it!

Herein lies the secret of nature. Behind its charming equanimity "is decay, which perfidiously conceals itself in order not to be seen for what it is . . ."[91] Its loveliness is always already susceptible to death, and, alas, "death is the stronger."[92] Thus the icon of nature has turned into a riddling doubt: "Is it life or death?"[93]

According to Kierkegaard, this question presses the onlooker to study nature more deeply and, in turn, to reconsider the words of Jesus: "No one can serve two masters." These words, he points out, prevent persons from merely dreaming about the lilies and the birds. Instead, they underline that the upshot of contemplation is a *krisis*, a decision to rest in God rather than in the world.

Here again the lilies and the birds image—both positively and negatively—this possibility. On the one hand, the natural world is faithful to God. Seasons do not fall out of order; the solar system does not deviate from its course. Moreover, these processes continue unabatedly. There is no stop and start, no wrestling with intentions, no thought of "what's in it for me." In short, nature knows but one master:

> Even though the lily does not serve God, it still serves only to God's honor. It does not spin, it does not work, it does not want to be anything at all itself or to have anything for itself, have it as plunder. The bird does not serve two masters. Even though it does not serve God, it exists only to God's honor, sings to his praise, does not demand at all to be anything itself.[94]

91. SKS 8, 298 / UDVS, 203.
92. SKS 8, 299 / UDVS, 203.
93. SKS 8, 299 / UDVS, 203.
94. SKS 8, 300 / UDVS, 205.

This fidelity intimates the human being's transparent rest in God. It is an icon of faith. And yet, as Kierkegaard goes on, there is a critical difference. Nature's constancy is not freely chosen but, rather, "bound in necessity."[95] In this way, its rest in God is different than that of the human being, for, as *The Sickness unto Death* makes clear, the self is a synthesis of necessity *and* freedom. In other words, the human being must *will* to rest transparently in God.

That the self has such a choice is its perfection. Not only does this excellence stem from the human being's singular constitution as a self-conscious synthesis of body and spirit, but it also signifies the "complaisance and indulgence"[96] of the one who established the human self. God is love, and love always grants the freedom by which one's individual circumstances derive significance. Kierkegaard illustrates this point with an analogy:

> What does the girl care about an inventory of all her fiancé's excellent qualities if she herself may not choose; and, on the other hand, whether others praise her beloved's many perfections or enumerate his faults, what more glorious thing could she say than when she says: He is my heart's choice![97]

Thus the human being is blessed with a choice between God and mammon. Even more blessed, however, is the *right* choice. Here again, according to Kierkegaard, the person can find guidance in the image of the lilies and the birds: "Only when the human being, although he works and spins, is just like the lily . . . only when the human being, although he sows and reaps and gathers into barns, is just like the bird . . . only then does he not serve mammon."[98]

95. SKS 8, 300 / UDVS, 205.
96. SKS 8, 301 / UDVS, 206.
97. SKS 8, 301 / UDVS, 206.
98. SKS 8, 303 / UDVS, 208.

The right choice, then, is God. It is right not simply because Scripture asserts it, but also because it satisfies the deepest needs of the self—that being of infinitude, which longs to transcend death's custody, that being of finitude, which seeks to find worth in *this* life. Happiness lies in the God who, creating and sustaining the world, nevertheless provides the means of its perfection.

In their own sort of faith, the lilies and the birds gesture toward this happiness, even as their otherness recalls the unique situation of the human being. The lilies and the birds will perish, but the self need not, if it only will turn from earthly despair and come to rest in God. Thus Kierkegaard concludes this discourse and, indeed, the entire treatise: "[I]f it was hard to live in want, then it must indeed be only an easier separation to die to want!"[99] The ultimate poverty of earthly life, the need for detachment, the joy of faith in God—this is a précis of Kierkegaard's spiritual thought, realized through his icon of the lilies in the field and the birds of the air.

The Ocean as Spiritual Icon

It should come as no surprise that, as a son of Denmark, Kierkegaard would draw on the ocean in his writings. Geographically, the nation is comprised of a peninsula and a seemingly countless number of islands, abutted by the North Sea in the north and west and the Baltic Sea in the south and east. Moreover, it is a traditional seafaring country, utilizing the ocean for fishing and, perhaps above all, trade. Kierkegaard's native city, Copenhagen, is a port on the eastern shore of the island of Zealand. Its name literally means "merchant's harbor."

For Kierkegaard, then, the ocean was practically ubiquitous, whether at home or in the countryside. When he journeyed through

99. SKS 8, 307 / UDVS, 212.

the woodlands of northern Zealand in 1835—a trip that was discussed earlier in this chapter—he also spent a great deal of time on the seacoast. In fact, he took up lodgings in the fishing village of Gilleleje, which served as a kind of "home base" during his stay. Kierkegaard described Gilleleje as "somewhat isolated,"[100] and he enjoyed walking along the beach up to Gilbjerg, the highest point in the area. There, with a "look of contemplation,"[101] he would reflect on the scene and on his life:

> Often, as I stood here on a quiet evening, the sea intoning its song with deep but calm solemnity, my eye catching not a single sail on the vast surface, and only the sea framed the sky and the sky the sea, while on the other hand the busy hum of life grew silent and the birds sang their vespers. . . . When the whole, seen thus in perspective, presented only the larger, bolder outlines and I didn't lose myself in detail as one so often does, but saw the whole in its totality, I gained the strength to grasp things differently, to admit how often I myself made mistakes, to forgive the mistakes of others. — As I stood there . . . alone and forsaken and the power of the sea and the battle of the elements reminded me of my nothingness, while the sure flight of the birds reminded me on the other hand of Christ's words, "Not a sparrow will fall to the earth without your heavenly Father's will," I felt at one and the same time how great and how insignificant I am.[102]

These reflections intimate the genesis of Kierkegaard's discourses on the lilies and the birds, but they also establish the ocean as an *objet de méditation* in its own right. For Kierkegaard, to see "the sea ruffled by a soft breeze" and "its surface transformed into a massive snowstorm" is to see "a sight that truly enjoins silence" and, with it, "true humility."[103] For whatever ambiguity surrounds Kierkegaard's parallel journal entry from Gilleleje[104]—in which he famously ponders

100. SKS 17, AA:10 / KJN 1, 13.
101. SKS 17, AA:6 / KJN 1, 9, my translation.
102. SKS 17, AA:6 / KJN 1, 9-10.
103. SKS 17, AA:6 / KJN 1, 10.
104. See Garff, *Kierkegaard*, 56-59.

"what the Deity really wants *me* to do . . . *the idea for which I am willing to live and die*"[105]—it is fitting that it, too, is attributed to his time on the coast. As will be seen, Kierkegaard consistently links the ocean with existential inquiry, spiritual development, and, finally, faith in God.

The first theme is evinced in Kierkegaard's "On the Occasion of a Confession," published in his 1845 collection, *Three Discourses on Imagined Occasions*. The subject of "On the Occasion of a Confession" is the meaning of seeking God. Kierkegaard begins by noting that the quest for God begins with an inchoate desire for the good. He likens this desire to a youthful sense of wonder, which muses on the existence of good things without knowing where to find them. This situation is especially true of the one who wonders about God, because God "is the highest, and yet the person wishing does not have a definite idea of it, because it is the highest as the unknown."[106] This divine darkness produces a "mixture of fear and blessedness"[107] akin to adoration; however, such an experience is not yet qualified in the Christian sense. It is "infinitely definable"[108] and, for that reason, can lead to the pantheism of paganism. It is with this possibility in mind that Kierkegaard turns to the ocean:

> When the ocean lies deep and still and inexplicable, when wonder stares dizzily down into it until it seems as if the unknown is rising to the surface, when the waves roll monotonously against the beach and overwhelm the soul by the power of the monotony . . . then [the pagan] worships.[109]

Thus the sea and other natural wonders, if considered in a certain way, lead to worship and even to idolatry. The worshipping person

105. SKS 17, AA:12 / KJN 1, 19.
106. SKS 5, 399 / TD, 18.
107. SKS 5, 399 / TD, 18.
108. SKS 5, 399 / TD, 18.
109. SKS 5, 400 / TD, 19.

can find God "everywhere in the least and the greatest."[110] Kierkegaard grants that this *habitus* is mistaken, but also suggests it is propaedeutic to true worship. As he puts it, "Wonder . . . is the beginning of all deeper understanding . . ."[111]

Here Kierkegaard hints at his concept of Religiousness A, which he was to develop in greater detail in *Concluding Unscientific Postscript to Philosophical Fragments*. Unlike Religiousness B—which Johannes Climacus identifies with Christianity—Religiousness A is intrinsic to human nature. In other words, it is not revealed *to* the human being but, rather, emerges *from* the person's search for what is transcendent and absolute. Consequently, the practitioner of Religiousness A seeks to contact the divine through finite, temporal existence. Despite the danger of lapsing into idolatry, Climacus insists that this search is crucial if the person is to advance to Religiousness B: "Religiousness *A* must first be present in the individual before there can be any consideration of becoming aware of the dialectical *B*."[112] The priority of Religiousness A should not be confused with superiority. Climacus's point, rather, is that the immanent search for God, born of wonder and a thirst for the highest good, stirs up a passion that is necessary for the reception of Christian truth.

Kierkegaard's pictures of the ocean, whether in his journals or in texts such as "On the Occasion of a Confession," certainly function in this way. They summon the very mystery of the natural world, with its ability to enchant the observer and to invite questions about the origin and nature of being. Elsewhere, however, Kierkegaard treats the ocean as an icon of the self's spiritual condition, capable of reflecting both despair and faith. A good example of the former is found in "The Seducer's Diary." As discussed in Chapter Three,

110. SKS 5, 400 / TD, 19.
111. SKS 5, 404 / TD, 24.
112. SKS 7, 506 / CUP1, 556.

the diary is attributed to the pseudonymous character, Johannes the Seducer, and it chronicles his pursuit of a young woman, Cordelia. In the secondary literature, Johannes is often described as an example of "detached, intellectual"[113] despair, since he is stimulated less by sexual craving than by the desire to manipulate his conquests spiritually. He *is* rapacious, but he violates the heart more than the body. As he writes after consummating his seduction:

> [I]t is finished, and I never want to see her again. When a girl has given away everything, she is weak, she has lost everything, for . . . innocence . . . in woman . . . is the substance of her being. Now all resistance is impossible, and to love is beautiful only as long as resistance is present; as soon as it ceases, to love is weakness and habit.[114]

And yet, for all of his icy calculation, it would be wrong to assume that Johannes lacks passion. On the contrary, the possibility of conquest stirs him deeply, only not in a visceral, erotic sense. It is *fantasy* that particularly arouses him, and, as long as his relationship remains imaginary, he is able to control and to relish it. He uses the ocean to picture his state of being:

> My mind roars like a turbulent sea in the storms of passion. If someone else could see my soul in this state, it would seem to him that it, like a skiff, plunged prow-first down into the ocean, as if in its dreadful momentum it would have to steer down into the depths of the abyss. He does not see that high on the mast a sailor is on the lookout. Roar away, you wild forces, roar away, you powers of passion; even if your waves hurl foam toward the clouds, you still are not able to pile yourselves up over my head—I am sitting as calmly as the king of the mountain.[115]

Here the ocean represents passion's fury, but Johannes casts himself as the sailor, who remains untouched by the tumult below. *He* is the

---

113. Watkin, *Kierkegaard's Philosophy*, 405.
114. SKS 2, 432 / EO1, 445.
115. SKS 2, 314 / EO1, 324–325.

master, conscious of what he is doing and why he is doing it. Thus he anticipates Anti-Climacus's portrayal of actively defiant despair, whereby the self "relates itself to itself only by way of imaginary constructions, no matter what it undertakes, however vast, however amazing, however perseveringly pursued."[116] Such a self is free—from others and, above all, from God—and "precisely this is the despair, but also what it regards as its pleasure and delight."[117] Johannes himself revels in the process of cultivating an identity, grooming a victim, taking advantage of her . . . and then starting over again. And yet, as Anti-Climacus maintains, this self-willed volatility is little more than a pretense, for a figure such as Johannes "is a king without a country, actually ruling over nothing."[118] Moreover, he is destined to end in the darkest abyss of despair: eventually "some difficulty" or some "basic defect" will thwart his protean abilities, thereby leading to a total embrace of "the demonic."[119] In other words—and to return to the image of the ocean—the tempestuous waters of the earthly life will one day topple the sailor. Climbing the mast of pure self-determination is an illusion, not a solution. Only a return to the harbor of faith can satisfy the self in the end.

Indeed, Kierkegaard does not think that the stormy sea, indicating the "struggle in [one's] own inner being,"[120] is the only way the ocean serves as a spiritual icon. On the contrary, he is more fond of treating the ocean as an image of spiritual *purity*. This approach surfaces in a journal entry from 1846, which reveals that he had been experimenting with the idea for some time: "Lyric over purity of heart, which is compared to the ocean."[121] This line, as it turns

---

116. SKS 11, 182 / SUD, 68.
117. SKS 11, 183 / SUD, 69.
118. SKS 11, 183 / SUD, 69.
119. SKS 11, 183–85 / SUD, 70–72.
120. SKS 8, 301 / UDVS, 205.
121. *Pap.* VII 1 B 173 / UDVS, 373.

out, refers to the opening treatise of *Upbuilding Discourses in Various Spirits*—"An Occasional Discourse," perhaps better known as "Purity of the Heart is to Will One Thing." It is in this text that Kierkegaard most fully and beautifully develops the iconic dimension of the ocean.

The "occasion" alluded to in the title, "An Occasional Discourse," is that of *confession*. Thus "An Occasional Discourse" recalls "On the Occasion of a Confession," discussed above. Both writings address the same attitude and context, and both invoke "stillness, wonder, and seeking God."[122] Howard and Edna Hong even claim that the earlier text "is extended in detail"[123] in the later one. Whatever the case, "An Occasional Discourse" begins with a remark about its purpose, which, given the nature of the present study, is as apropos as it is intriguing. Kierkegaard compares his authorial task to that of a seamstress, who "works on a cloth for sacred use."[124] The seamstress by no means disdains the attempt to make her art beautiful. However, its beauty is to serve as a channel by which the observer comes into contact with the holy, not as an object of contemplation in and of itself. The seamstress would be "deeply distressed if anyone were to make the mistake of seeing her artistry instead of the meaning of the cloth or were to make the mistake of seeing a defect instead of seeing the meaning of the cloth."[125] Rather, the seamstress and her skill are to be detached from, even "infinitely forgotten."[126] Only then, when the observer has withdrawn from accidental considerations and become attentive to "himself and his own self,"[127] can the artistry function as a spiritual icon.

122. Howard and Edna Hong, "Historical Introduction," in *Three Discourses on Imagined Occasions*, ed. and trans. Howard V. Hong and Edna H. Hong (Princeton, NJ: Princeton University Press, 1993), x.
123. Ibid.
124. SKS 8, 121 / UDVS, 5.
125. SKS 8, 121 / UDVS, 5.
126. SKS 8, 121 / UDVS, 5.
127. SKS 8, 121 / UDVS, 5.

Likewise, a certain attitude is needed to see Kierkegaard's pictures of the ocean rightly. Yet, if this attitude is cultivated, the observer will be able to perceive the holy. Kierkegaard later refers to this state of mind as "quietness,"[128] though he is at pains to distinguish the quietness of a "wistful mood" [*veemodige Stemning*][129] from the quietness of standing in earnest before God. He uses the ocean to illustrate each of these dispositions.

There is, he begins, something lovely about stepping off "the noisy main highway" and entering into "the quiet places."[130] All alone, the person "feels . . . as if something ineffable forced its way out of his innermost being," a feeling that is akin to longing and yet still beyond it, since "even *longing* . . . is not the inexpressible itself—it is only hastening after it."[131] In this silence, a sense of wonder is kindled. The person seems to be watched as much as he is watching. Everything moves, yet nothing speaks, and "what the surroundings are saying with this quietness: that is the inexpressible."[132] It is the same with the sea:

> And the ocean, like the wise man, is self-sufficient, whether it lies just like a child and amuses itself by itself with gentle ripples, like a child playing on its lips, or at midday lies, like a half-sleeping indulgent thinker, surveying everything around it, or at night it deeply ponders its own nature; whether with profound subtlety it makes itself into nothing in order to observe or it rages in its own passion. The ocean runs deep, it indeed knows what it knows; the one who runs deep always knows that, but it has no co-knowledge.[133]

This mysteriousness is inviting: "Walk along the beach and let the movement of the ocean accompany the indefiniteness of your

128. SKS 8, 134 / UDVS, 20.
129. SKS 8, 136 / UDVS, 21, my translation.
130. SKS 8, 135 / UDVS, 20.
131. SKS 8, 135 / UDVS, 20.
132. SKS 8, 135 / UDVS, 20.
133. SKS 8, 135 / UDVS, 20–21.

thoughts—but do not stand still, do not discover the uniformity; if you hear it for just a half second, it is already difficult to tear yourself away from this spell."[134] And yet, it is also frustrating. The person captivated by the secrets of the ocean—or those of nature in general—listens for answers. But the ocean carries on, and "the traveler at its side only grows older."[135]

It is different for the one who is confessing. The one who desires to confess before God does not merely happen upon quietness, as a walker stumbles upon a solitary meadow. Nor does the one confessing seek out quietness as such, for ambience is not needed but, rather, the opportunity to collect oneself before God. Kierkegaard says the quietness of confession bears "the earnestness of eternity,"[136] and it is through such a silence that one can come to *will the good alone*."[137] Kierkegaard calls this state "purity of heart,"[138] and he adds—following the Sermon on the Mount, but also in a manner evocative of Christian mysticism—that this purity is a necessary precursor to encountering the divine presence.

Purity of heart, then, consists of a single-minded willing of the good. Thus it excludes what Kierkegaard, drawing on the Epistle of James,[139] terms "*double-mindedness*."[140] As Kierkegaard explains it, double-mindedness is the simultaneous pursuit of multifarious aims. This sort of willing is obvious when, say, one wants both money and prestige. Yet, notes Kierkegaard, it is also present whenever a person desires something as broad as "pleasure," for "the unity of pleasure is a delusion and a deception."[141] To will pleasure is to will a variety of

---

134. SKS 18, JJ:398 / JP 3, 2836.
135. SKS 8, 136 / UDVS, 21.
136. SKS 8, 136 / UDVS, 21.
137. SKS 8, 138 / UDVS, 24, my translation.
138. SKS 8, 138 / UDVS, 24.
139. See James 4:8.
140. SKS 8, 138 / UDVS, 24.
141. SKS 8, 141 / UDVS, 27.

pleasures, since pleasure is contingent and therefore ephemeral. Now it lies in this, now in that: "Change was what he called for when pleasure served him—change, change; and change was what he called for when he arrived at the limits of pleasure, when the servants were exhausted—change, change!"[142] Just as a child plays with one toy for a while, tosses it aside and then moves on to another toy, so does the one who seeking pleasure make "variation . . . his watchword."[143]

But what is wrong with such variation? Kierkegaard offers a number of answers. First, multifarious willing indicates that the person "is also divided in himself."[144] The self, in other words, has no unifying ground. This deficiency, at least in part, has to do with *what* the self is seeking. An esteemed career, an impressive home, a string of sexual conquests—no matter how much enjoyment these bring, the enjoyment cannot last. "[T]he worldly is not one thing; multifarious as it is, in life it is changed into its opposite, in death into nothing, in eternity into a curse . . ."[145] Even worse, this lack of unity and its constant buffeting of the self is tantamount to despair: "[I]s not despair actually double-mindedness; or what else is it to despair but to have two wills!"[146] Here Kierkegaard is making a play on words. An old Danish word for "two" [*Tvende*, shortened to *Tv-*] is implicit in both "double-mindedness" [*Tvesindethed*] and "despair" [*Fortvivelse*]. Indeed, *Fortvivelse* can be broken into two component words: "of" [*for*] and "doubt" [*tvivl*]. Thus despair is an extreme kind of doubt, which is itself a "twoness." This sickness can take on any number of forms—the person who wills the good out of fear, the person who wills the good for the sake of personal gain, the person who wills the

142. SKS 8, 141 / UDVS, 27.
143. SKS 8, 141 / UDVS, 27.
144. SKS 8, 141 / UDVS, 27.
145. SKS 8, 143 / UDVS, 28–29.
146. SKS 8, 144 / UDVS, 30.

good to an extent. In each case, the self is riven, wrenched in a variety of directions. There is no self-integration, no *rest*.

With this point established, Kierkegaard turns to purity of heart. This ideal, he argues, is possible only if the person wills the good (which is one) and does so in truth (which involves a total commitment). But what, exactly, does purity of heart *look* like? Kierkegaard concedes that it "is a metaphorical expression,"[147] which is best understood in such terms. The most apt comparison, he goes on to explain, is to the ocean, because the ocean is capable of depth and of transparency:

> [T]he ocean's depth is its purity, and its purity is its transparency, because the ocean is deep only when it is pure, and pure only when it is transparent. As soon as it is impure, it is not deep but shallow, and as soon as it is shallow it is not transparent either. When, however, it is deeply and transparently pure, then, however long one continues to look at it, it is one thing; then its purity in this constancy is one thing. That is why we compare the heart to the ocean, because its purity is this constancy in being deep and in being transparent. No storm may agitate it, no sudden gust of wind may move its surface; no drowsy fog may spread over it; there must be no dubious [*tvivlsom*] movement within it; no fleeting cloud may darken it; but it must lie still, deeply transparent. And if you see it this way today, you are uplifted by beholding [*at skue*] the ocean's purity, and if you see it this way every day, then you say it is constantly pure—like the heart of someone who wills only one thing.[148]

This quiet purity is not a quality intrinsic to the ocean itself. Rather, it is a reflection of the sky above, whose own tranquility is mirrored in the sea below. Indeed, "[i]f the least thing comes between them,

147. SKS 8, 222 / UDVS, 121.
148. SKS 8, 222 / UDVS, 121. I have slightly amended this translation. The Hongs translate *at skue* as "gazing at." This rendering is not inconceivable, though it is hardly the most direct translation. Indeed, *at skue* literally means "to behold"—a word that, following Marion, avoids the idolatrous connotations of "gazing." After all, "behold" is etymologically related to "belong," which carries with it the undertones of "membership" and "unity." In this way, it better accords with Kierkegaard's intention, which does not stress a mere staring at the ocean but, rather, an echoing of the ocean's purity in the "uplifted" observer.

between the sky and the ocean . . . then the ocean is not pure, then it does not purely reflect the sky."[149] So, when the wind whips up and the "ocean rages in storm and the sky is hidden,"[150] purity is lost, despite the fact that ocean and sky "blend as one in the turmoil."[151] This loss is because purity is not just any kind of unity. Thus Kierkegaard distinguishes between unity-in-confusion and unity-in-distinction.[152] The former is won through force and results in distortion, whereas the latter involves the harmonious concord of contraries. The former violates otherness; the latter preserves it. As Kierkegaard explains, "Not until they are distinguished in peace, when the sky arches high over the ocean, which deeply reflects it, not until then do we say that it is pure."[153]

The same, Kierkegaard notes, is true of the person who wills the good in purity and in truth:

> [J]ust as the ocean becomes pure when it aspires only to heaven, so the heart becomes pure when it aspires only to the good. Just as the ocean reflects the height of heaven in its pure depth, so the heart, when it is still and deeply transparent, reflects in its pure depth the heavenly sublimity of the good.[154]

It is at this point that the connection between purity of heart and Anti-Climacus's faith becomes unmistakable. As has been discussed, Anti-Climacus understands faith as "transparent rest" in God. It is a way of being—in contradistinction to a mere cognitive assent to doctrine—in which the human being self-consciously wills to be what God wills her to be. In other words, faith coordinates the human being with God. The two opposites are united, not in such

---

149. SKS 8, 222 / UDVS, 121.
150. *Pap.* VII 1 B 192:13 / JP 4, 4435.
151. *Pap.* VII 1 B 192:13 / JP 4, 4435.
152. *Pap.* VII 1 B 192:13 / JP 4, 4435.
153. *Pap.* VII 1 B 192:13 / JP 4, 4435.
154. SKS 8, 222 / UDVS, 121.

a way that they are ontologically blurred, but in such a way that the lesser (the self) is harmonized with the greater ("the power that established it"). Faith, then, is a kind of purity of heart, or, more precisely, it is the decisive form of purity of heart. It is the elimination of double-mindedness (despair, sin) and, with it, the single-minded willing of that which God wills—namely, the good.

Once more, Kierkegaard turns to the natural word to illustrate his spiritual thought. The ocean is the ocean, and yet it is more than that. Its play of light, waves, and wind bears a picture of the human self, caught up in its own play of infinity and finitude, of freedom and necessity. Above all, if one sees the ocean on a calm day, when sea and sky mirror one another, distinct yet one in mutual placidity, it images the faith by which the human being roots out despair and finds joy in God.

Conclusion

When Kierkegaard eschewed a vocation as a naturalist for one as a writer, he reasoned that he simply could not view nature as so much matter: "I am reminded of the sounds of the spiritual world . . . the departure of the migratory birds reminds me of the more profound yearnings of the human heart."[155] This chapter has borne out Kierkegaard's rationale. Time and again it has been seen that, for Kierkegaard, natural forms such as trees, wind, color, birds, flowers, and water convey rich spiritual meaning. They become, in his hands, icons of the self as it pursues happiness—a happiness that, as his pictures often show, is realized only in and through the self's transparent rest in God. This rest is faith.

155. SKS 17, AA:12 / LD, 45.

And yet, Kierkegaard's handling of nature is hardly unique in his authorship. On the contrary, it exemplifies a method he was to apply elsewhere, particularly in his treatment of certain biblical figures. Indeed, like so many great Christian artists, Kierkegaard repeatedly portrays biblical characters as icons of faith, tendered for the sake of contemplation. The fifth and final chapter of this study will explore these biblical figures and show how they signify what Kierkegaard understands as the richness of faith's unfolding life.

5

Icons of Faith:
The Bible

Though typically thought of as a religion of the book, as a faith in the Word,[1] Christianity has long had a place for the image. The Eastern Church locates the origin of Christian iconography to the time of Jesus Christ himself. According to legend, King Abgar of Edessa sent one of his servants to Palestine in the hope of persuading Jesus to visit him. A leper, the king anticipated the Savior would be able to heal him. Jesus was unable to make the journey, but the servant did not return empty-handed. He brought the king a cloth that bore Jesus' image—the result, so it goes, of Jesus drying his face on the fabric. In the presence of this likeness, Abgar was healed, and the cloth was revered as a sacred relic, indeed, as the first icon. It is for that reason that the great Russian iconographer Léonid Ouspensky could say, "Christianity is the revelation not only of the Word of God but also the Image of God."[2]

The import of this statement is reflected in the various rules of icon painting. For example, icons are not to be treated as works of art;

1. See, for example, John 1:1: "In the beginning was the Word [*Logos*], and the Word was with God, and the Word was God."
2. Quoted in Jim Forest, *Praying with Icons* (Maryknoll, NY: Orbis Books, 2008), 3.

rather, they are aids to worship, drawing the observer "beyond what can be seen . . . into the realm of mystical experience."[3] This self-effacement is literally etched into the structure of icons. They are not to imply sound of any kind, so as to foster the silence necessary for contemplative prayer.[4] Likewise, they are to supply only a minimal amount of detail. Settings are either foregone or "rendered in the simplest, most austere manner."[5] Thus icons are, in a key sense, *abstract*—a term that literally means "drawn away." Since the divine is inexhaustible, icons must detach from precise, technical depictions and instead embrace evocation. To cite Ouspensky again, "Spiritual reality cannot be represented in any other way except through symbols."[6]

These guidelines apply to the *painting* of icons, though icons need not be confined to a single medium. As alluded to in Chapter Three, Jean-Luc Marion argues that an icon is more than a kind of art; it is also a "manner of being."[7] That is not to say that, for Marion, icons lack any determinate content. As he puts it, "Even if the number of those [icons] that demand veneration and the mode of that veneration vary, all admit nevertheless to certain common minimal characteristics: it is a question of *signa* concerning the divine."[8] In other words, icons are signs of divinity, and signs are as proper to language as to image. Icon painting "presents one of the possible media,"[9] but hardly the only one. As Marion goes on, "[T]he icon also can proceed conceptually, provided at least that the concept renounce comprehending the incomprehensible, to attempt to conceive it, hence also to receive it, in its own excessiveness."[10] Hence, whether

3. Ibid., 18.
4. Ibid.
5. Ibid., 19.
6. Quoted in ibid., 18.
7. Jean-Luc Marion, *God Without Being* (Chicago: University of Chicago Press, 1991), 7.
8. Ibid., 8.
9. Ibid., 22.

in concepts or in pictures, "the concept of distance" must be present in icons, albeit in such a way that the "absolute distinction" between the visible and the invisible terminates in "the radical commerce of their transferences."[11] Only then do icons realize their ultimate purpose—namely, to facilitate "union,"[12] to encourage a way of being *with* the divine.

This existential orientation is consonant with traditional iconography. As Gennadios Limouris writes, "The true content of the icon . . . is a real spiritual orientation of the Christian life and, in particular, of Christian prayer."[13] The icon literally *in-forms* one's interaction with the world. It opens up the "spiritual microcosm . . . towards the macrocosm of the universe."[14]

Kierkegaard's writings display a number of these iconographic qualities. As has been discussed, a significant portion of his authorship is dedicated to "upbuilding," his preferred term for spiritual growth. This commitment not only entails a rhetorically adept, maieutic elicitation of such growth, but also requires Kierkegaard to address many of the key themes of the Christian spiritual tradition—for example, the absolute transcendence of God, the creation and fall of the human person, as well as the person's spiritual journey back to God and, in turn, to happiness. Moreover, it has been shown that Kierkegaard not only develops such themes in discursive fashion, but renders them in pictorial form. These "icons of faith," as I have called them, symbolize Kierkegaard's spiritual thought, providing the reader with images of the self's quest for and attainment of the happy rest of faith. Broadly speaking, Kierkegaard's icons fall under one of

10. Ibid., 22–23.
11. Ibid., 23.
12. Ibid.
13. Gennadios Limouris, "The Microcosm and Macrocosm of the Icon: Theology, Spirituality and Worship in Colour," in *Icons: Windows on Eternity: Theology and Spirituality in Color*, compiled by Gennadios Limouris (Geneva: WCC Publications, 1990), 118.
14. Ibid.

two categories—those of the natural world and those of figures from the Bible. Chapter Four dealt with the former; the task of this chapter is to expound on the latter.

In one sense, then, the aim of this chapter is more straightforward than its predecessor. After all, iconography has traditionally used biblical personages as subjects. In this connection, one need only think of the countless images of the crucified Christ and the Virgin and Child, not to mention icons of Old Testament personages such as Moses, David, and, perhaps most famously, Andrei Rublev's *The Old Testament Trinity*. That Kierkegaard, too, features biblical figures in his writings—explicitly treating them as pictures for contemplation—marks him as an inheritor of this tradition. To consider his icons, it would seem, is primarily a matter of considering the historical figures or biblical events he is picturing.

But this view, while not entirely inapt, fails to do justice to the complexity of Kierkegaard's efforts. As will be seen, Kierkegaard's icons are not mere renderings of ancient saints and the like. They also embody his unique reading of the biblical message, so that to contemplate them is, at the same time, to envision Kierkegaard's understanding of Christian spirituality. In short, what Kierkegaard develops conceptually in works such as *The Sickness unto Death* he represents iconically in other writings. This point should not imply that Kierkegaard's icons of biblical persons are somehow unbiblical. Rather, it is to say that they are *also* windows into his own thought, giving particular access to his treatment of concepts such as "faith" and "sin." As Timothy Houston Polk writes, "Kierkegaard does not so much talk *about* the Bible as kaleidoscopically *use* it."[15] Here Polk's employment of the term "kaleidoscopically" is felicitous, for "kaleidoscope" literally means "observer of beautiful forms." In his

---

15. Timothy Houston Polk, *The Biblical Kierkegaard: Reading by the Rule of Faith* (Macon, GA: Mercer University Press, 1997), 17.

icons, which are indeed reproductions of biblical forms, Kierkegaard develops what he sees as the beauty of the Christian spiritual journey.

With this in mind, another peculiar feature of Kierkegaard's biblical icons emerges—namely, his tendency to highlight marginal, even offbeat characters. Though he certainly displays an interest in major figures such as Abraham, John the Baptist, and Jesus Christ, he also depicts three lesser persons from the Gospel of Luke—Anna, the tax collector, and the woman who was a sinner. The latter, in fact, he treats in three different discourses, arguably making her, apart from Christ, Kierkegaard's favorite subject. Other icons include Job, the Apostle Peter, and Paul of Tarsus, adding further variety to Kierkegaard's gallery of pictures. These figures, as will be seen, symbolize an aspect of faith. Thus they not only bring nuance to Kierkegaard's thought but indicate the very richness of the Christian spiritual life.

With so many characters available, it would be unwieldy to detail each of them in full. Here, then, the task is more modest. Proceeding from the prior argument that faith, as transparent rest in God, is the foundation of Kierkegaard's spirituality, this chapter will show how Kierkegaard locates faith in certain biblical figures and, thereby, elucidates what faith entails. Three aspects of faith will garner specific attention: (i) faith as humility, (ii) faith as suffering, and (iii) faith as love. These attributes will be treated in turn, with various figures serving to represent the given theme.

Nevertheless, this approach should not imply that faith can somehow be divided up—for Kierkegaard understands faith precisely as wholeness—nor should it suggest that one can have a "humble faith" without a "loving faith" and so on. On the contrary, there will be significant overlap between these different aspects, since, for Kierkegaard, humility requires a willingness to suffer, suffering a vocation to love, and love a rootedness in humility. But this correspondence is as it should be. Though their stories differ, though they belong to different classes, eras, or genders, each of the figures depicted by Kierkegaard is united by a common quality—*faith*. To contemplate them is to contemplate why, for Kierkegaard, faith is the decisive moment in the journey of Christian spirituality.

Faith as Humility

Kierkegaard's publication of *Two Upbuilding Discourses* in May 1843 was one of the defining moments of his career. Coming on the heels of *Either/Or*—a poetic-cum-philosophical magnum opus, which created a "sensation"[16] in literary circles upon its release a few months earlier—*Two Upbuilding Discourses* revealed the complexity of Kierkegaard's authorial mission. He would not be content to issue avant-garde pseudonymous works, nor would he sacrifice substance for popularity—a point confirmed by the paltry sales figures of his six volumes of upbuilding writings.[17] Rather, he wanted to develop an oeuvre dedicated to religious awakening. As he later explained in *On My Work as an Author*, "'*Without authority*' to make aware of the religious, the essentially Christian, is the category for my whole work as an author regarded as a totality."[18]

The release of *Two Upbuilding Discourses* can be seen as confirmation of this intention, for it initiated the "pattern"[19] that characterized much of Kierkegaard's literary career—namely, the almost simultaneous release of pseudonymous works and signed upbuilding discourses.[20] Both sets of writings were to elicit "religious

16. Howard V. Hong and Edna H. Hong, "Historical Introduction," in *Eighteen Upbuilding Discourses*, ed. Howard V. Hong and Edna H. Hong (Princeton, NJ: Princeton University Press, 1990), xvii.
17. Ibid., xxi.
18. SKS 13, 19 / PV, 12.
19. Hong and Hong, "Historical Introduction," ix.

commitment,"[21] but in different modes. Whereas the pseudonymous texts "present and discuss different views of life," thereby prompting the reader "to consider the truth of these different views and their relevance to his or her life,"[22] the signed discourses "are modeled on contemporary sermons" and thus "presume that the reader is someone who is serious about living religiously."[23] The former are more literary, the latter more hortatory.

Kierkegaard himself provides another way of expressing this difference. He distinguishes between strategies of communication, the pseudonymous writings representing an "indirect" method, the upbuilding ones a "direct" approach.[24] He uses a metaphor to contrast these two ways. Likening the reader to a jar, he states that indirect communication presupposes that the jar has to be *emptied* before it can be filled with something new. Direct communication, on the other hand, assumes the reader is *ready* to be filled.[25] Thus his signed, direct discourses supply the content with which the "jar" is filled.

With this point in mind, it is telling that the short prayer inaugurating *Two Upbuilding Discourses*—and, with it, Kierkegaard's pattern of issuing signed discourses in conjunction with pseudonymous works—alludes to the iconic dimension of his authorship. Speaking of the need for reassurance in the Christian life, Kierkegaard writes,

> [W]hen in mournful moments we want to strengthen and encourage our minds by contemplating those great men, your chosen instruments, who in severe spiritual trials and anxieties of heart kept their minds free,

20. Ibid., ix–x.
21. SKS 22, NB14:31, 362 / JP 6, 6533.
22. Julia Watkin, *Historical Dictionary of Kierkegaard's Philosophy* (Lanham, MD: Scarecrow Press, 2001), 6.
23. George Pattison, foreword to *Kierkegaard: Spiritual Writings*, trans. George Pattison (New York: Harper Perennial, 2010), xiii.
24. SKS 13, 14 / PV, 8.
25. SKS 13, 14 / PV, 8.

their courage uncrushed, and heaven open, we, too, wish to add our witness to theirs in the assurance that even if our courage compared with theirs is only discouragement, our power powerlessness, you, however, are still the same, the same mighty God. . . .[26]

Here, then, Kierkegaard identifies the contemplation of biblical figures as an important aspect of Christian devotion. In doing so, he also implies that his own authorship is a means to that end—a place where such figures can be encountered and pondered. Finally, he suggests that what unites the contemplator and the contemplated is God himself, whose eternal sameness animates all who "trust"[27] in him, even (or especially) those who are aware of their own weakness.

Thus faith proceeds from a fundamental humility. Even though it is "the highest good, the most beautiful, the most precious,"[28] it cannot be had without humility. In fact, as Kierkegaard sees it, humility is implicit in the very nature of faith. For faith's greatness lies in a kind of ordinariness: unlike money, prestige, or talent, faith is available to all persons. As Kierkegaard explains,

> [F]aith is qualitatively different. It is not only the highest good, but it is a good in which all are able to share, and the person who rejoices in the possession of it also rejoices in the countless human race, "because what I possess," he says, "every human being has or can possess."[29]

It follows, then, that Kierkegaard's "icons of faith" will register something of this humility—a word whose root is the Latin *humus* or "earth." The humble person will not exalt herself but, rather, remain *humilis* ("on the ground"). This is a *double entendre*. For Kierkegaard, to be humble is to be grounded not only in the sense of recognizing one's own creaturely limitations, but also in the sense of being

---

26. SKS 5, 17 / EUD, 7.
27. SKS 5, 17 / EUD, 7.
28. SKS 5, 19 / EUD, 9.
29. SKS 5, 20 / EUD, 10.

grounded in God. Both meanings are evident in Kierkegaard's icons of the humility of faith, including, as will be described below, John the Baptist and the tax collector.[30]

John the Baptist

Kierkegaard treats John the Baptist in "He Must Increase; I Must Decrease," the third and final discourse from *Three Upbuilding Discourses* (1844). The title is taken from a passage in the Gospel of

---

30. Here is as good a place as any to mention Kierkegaard's treatment of Abraham, particularly in the (in)famous 1845 work *Fear and Trembling*. Attributed to the pseudonym, Johannes *de silentio* [John of Silence], *Fear and Trembling* certainly bears a resemblance to Kierkegaard's other "iconographic" writings. It concerns a biblical figure, Abraham, who is heralded as an archetype of faith, "that power whose strength is powerlessness" (SKS 4, 113 / FT, 16). Indeed, for that reason, Johannes implores his reader to approach Abraham as a kind of icon: "It is human to lament, human to weep with one who weeps, but it is greater to have faith, more blessed to contemplate the man of faith" (SKS 4, 114 / FT, 17). At first blush, then, it would seem fitting to include a section on Abraham in this chapter. In truth, however, *Fear and Trembling* would constitute an *exception* (albeit a fascinating one) to the works treated in this study and so would be best analyzed in another context. Two main reasons account for this difference: (i) that of authorship and (ii) that of intention. In the first case, *Fear and Trembling* is a pseudonymous text, whereas most of the other writings discussed here are signed discourses. Moreover, even as far as pseudonymous works are concerned, a distinction is involved, since Johannes *de silentio* is not at all like, say, Anti-Climacus. The latter Kierkegaard regards as a Christian *par excellence*, while Johannes *de silentio* repeatedly acknowledges his confusion about faith (SKS 4, 103 / FT, 7) and, indeed, his own lack of faith (SKS 4, 143–44 / FT, 50–51). Thus Johannes's picture of Abraham, while intriguing, is incomplete and even one-sided: it says more about *him* than about faith. This point leads to the second reason for omitting *Fear and Trembling* in this context—namely, its aim (which is ordinary among Kierkegaard's pseudonymous writings) to lay bare an aesthetic *Weltanschauung*, rather than to upbuild directly. Doubtless *Fear and Trembling* is a stimulating work, but, as Ronald Green notes, it presents one with an appalling image of Abraham, an "exemplar [who] borders on the psychopathic" (Ronald M. Green, "'Developing' *Fear and Trembling*," in *The Cambridge Companion to Kierkegaard*, ed. Alastair Hannay and Gordon D. Marino [Cambridge: Cambridge University Press, 1998], 268). Green himself grants that "this may be part of Kierkegaard's purpose in troubling his contemporaries' religious complacency," and he adds that the text "may point to another, and still deeper, level of meaning" (Ibid., 268). Be that as it may—and I personally agree that *Fear and Trembling* is far more nuanced than often acknowledged—Green's point nevertheless supports the exclusion of *Fear and Trembling* in this context. Johannes *de silentio*, first and foremost, gestures toward the darkness of faith from the side of a non-believer. Such an approach has its place, and may reward attempts to decode its "secret ink" (Ibid., 258), but the one seeking faith's happy rest in God best start elsewhere in Kierkegaard's oeuvre.

John, which tells of how John the Baptist's disciples confronted him about the newfound popularity of Jesus, whose ministry was growing in inverse proportion to John's. Yet, rather than express jealousy, John responded that he ministered at the pleasure of God, who had seen fit for him to prepare the way for the Messiah. For that reason, John said he was pleased with Jesus' success, just as one is happy at the wedding of a friend: "[M]y joy has been fulfilled. He must increase, but I must decrease" (John 3:29-30).

John's story is a unique one, and yet, notes Kierkegaard, this particular aspect of it overlaps with a common human experience—namely, the recognition that one is no longer the best or the highest at something:

> Who does not know that things like these have happened and do happen in the world—that someone who once ruled over countries and kingdoms has ceased to rule and is obliged to see a more powerful ruler take his place; . . . that the master whose pupil only yesterday sat at his feet must bow his shoulders today under the other's advancement; . . . that the girl who once filled her beloved's thoughts now sits and sees his bold ambition pursuing a higher goal; that the singer whose words were on everyone's lips is forgotten today and his songs have been more than replaced. . . .[31]

The person who has faced such circumstances may seek guidance from "those distinguished people whose memory the generations have preserved," but John's witness is special even among biblical figures. For John is differentiated by his task "to be reconciled—to being forgotten."[32] He is called to celebrate his own decline. In this way, he is an icon of faith's *humble self-denial*.[33]

To consider this quality is, according to Kierkegaard, to see an authentic way of being-in-the-world. In other words, humble self-

31. SKS 5, 272 / EUD, 278–79.
32. SKS 5, 273 / EUD, 279.
33. SKS 5, 275 / EUD, 279.

denial is not an end in itself but, rather, a manifestation of faith's internal harmony. Kierkegaard elaborates on this point in a few ways. First, he points out that John's humility allows him to understand himself as a tool in God's hands. "Every human being is only an instrument," notes Kierkegaard, and if one "does not at times evoke this thought," one is simply trying to avoid "the uncertainty in which he comprehends his own nothingness."[34] In faith, however, John grasps his own contingency, and it is precisely this recognition that allows him to serve God and others. Simply put, he is free. As Kierkegaard explains, "[T]he thought of being dismissed liberates the servant to be one of God's co-workers, just as the thought of death liberates a person, saves him from being a bond servant who wants to belong only to the earth, from being a cheat who does not want to belong to God."[35]

Next, Kierkegaard states that John's self-effacement testifies to his willingness to be *himself*. After all, there are other possibilities. On the one hand, he could fantastically view himself as the Messiah and, therefore, his own work as more important than that of Jesus. On the other hand, he could doubt whether a poor and reclusive person such as himself could be *actually* associated with the Son of God. But he does not succumb to either form of despair. Rather, he accepts his peculiar station in life, thereby evincing a "humble self-denial [that] remains true to itself."[36] Kierkegaard illustrates this point by imagining John with his followers:

> In their eyes he was still the great one; they were accustomed to hail him as master. Secretly they perhaps had nourished the thought that he himself was the one who was to come. . . . Now he has made his appearance—the expected one—and the disheartened disciples trusted that the news they were bringing to the Baptizer would elicit from him

34. SKS 5, 275 / EUD, 282.
35. SKS 5, 275 / EUD, 282.
36. SKS 5, 278 / EUD, 285.

the desired explanation. The expected one had come; the Baptizer could have . . . hidden himself in an out-of-the-way place with his disciples, and in their eyes continued to be the master.[37]

But John does nothing of the kind. Instead, he remains "true to [himself]"[38] and thus stands as an icon of humble faith. As Kierkegaard implores, "How beneficial it is to contemplate what is worthy of veneration!"[39]

Finally, Kierkegaard attends to John's happiness, his "self-denying joy."[40] This is a key distinction, because Kierkegaard is at pains to note that John's happiness is not an "emotion . . . quick to melt into sentimental moods."[41] In other words, his is not a "false feeling," but a "discriminating judgment of truth."[42] He recognizes that "[n]o one can receive anything except what has been given from heaven" (John 3:27), and, thus resting in "the chasmic abyss"[43] between God and himself, he rejoices in what is true, in what is *real*. Like the "the bridegroom's friend,"[44] who realizes the nature of his role, John rejoices at stepping aside.

As the wedding metaphor makes clear, John's example is by no means discontinuous with ordinary human experience. On the contrary, it applies to a number of situations in life, and, for that reason, one ought to "contemplate" his image frequently and so grow "intimate" with it.[45] This contemplation is a means of inward deepening, drawing one into a kind of spiritual journey—a journey that, according to Kierkegaard, culminates in a "new joy," which

37. SKS 5, 276–77 / EUD, 283.
38. SKS 5, 278 / EUD, 285.
39. SKS 5, 277 / EUD, 283–84.
40. SKS 5, 278 / EUD, 285.
41. SKS 5, 278 / EUD, 286.
42. SKS 5, 278 / EUD, 286.
43. SKS 5, 279 / EUD, 286.
44. SKS 5, 281 / EUD, 287.
45. SKS 5, 280 / EUD, 288.

"will surely be full."[46] Utterly unique, yet happily familiar, this is the new joy of faith.

The Tax Collector

Kierkegaard's second collection of eucharistic discourses, *Three Discourses at the Communion on Fridays*, was published on November 14, 1849. Less than four months earlier, Kierkegaard had issued *The Sickness unto Death*, and he intended *Three Discourses at the Communion on Fridays* to serve as a signed "companion volume"[47] to that pseudonymous work. Their companionship can be taken in two ways. First, Kierkegaard notes that, as he pondered the end of his literary career, he did not want to conclude his authorship with a pseudonymous writing: "I must have a place of rest, but I cannot use a pseudonym as a place of rest . . ."[48] Second, he maintains that the writings comprising *Three Discourses at the Communion on Fridays* are not only "related to the last pseudonym, Anti-Climacus,"[49] but "are parallel to Anti-Climacus."[50] These two ways are intertwined. Kierkegaard did not want to end his authorship with a pseudonym because he wanted to underscore that *he*, Søren Kierkegaard, was a religious author.[51] In turn, he sought to translate Anti-Climacus's abstract prose into the iconographic treatises of *Three Discourses at the Communion on Fridays*, so that the "stress [might] be in the direction of upbuilding."[52] The signed discourses, in short, picture the insights of their predecessor.

46. SKS 5, 281 / EUD, 289.
47. Howard V. Hong and Edna H. Hong, "Historical Introduction," in *Without Authority*, ed. Howard V. Hong and Edna H. Hong (Princeton, NJ: Princeton University Press, 1997), xv.
48. SKS 22, NB13:79 / JP 6, 6519.
49. SKS 22, NB13:57 / JP 6, 6515.
50. SKS 22, NB13:79 / JP 6, 6519.
51. SKS 22, NB13:79 / JP 6, 6519.
52. SKS 22, NB13:79 / JP 6, 6519.

With this in mind, it should not be surprising that the second treatise in *Three Discourses at the Communion on Fridays*, "The Tax Collector," stands as an icon of the humility of faith. The discourse draws on Luke 18:13, wherein Jesus tells of a publican who, conscious of his sins, entreats God for mercy. Jesus contrasts this figure with a Pharisee, who proclaimed himself righteous and even thanked God that he was unlike sinners such as the tax collector. Interestingly, the sincerity of the Pharisee's piety is never doubted by Jesus; indeed, he grants that the Pharisee fasts, tithes, and so on (18:12). The trouble, however, has to do with the Pharisee's understanding of faith. For him, faith is not a way of being—an interior state characterized by modesty—but a means of elevating himself above others. Thus he misconstrues *what* faith is and, in turn, fails to understand *who* he is.

As he opens "The Tax Collector," Kierkegaard makes clear that the question of self-understanding lies at the core of the parable. In other words, Jesus is not warning against this or that behavior; rather, he is stressing the necessity of properly knowing oneself in relation to God. That this lesson is all too easily missed, Kierkegaard adds, is evinced by the fact that many recent Christians haughtily distinguish themselves from the Pharisee:

> [Some persons] "trust in themselves that they are righteous and despise others," while they nevertheless fashion their character in the likeness of the tax collector and sanctimoniously stand far off. . . . These are hypocrites who, just as the Pharisee blasphemously said in his prayer, "God, I thank you that I am not like this tax collector," sanctimoniously say, "God, I thank you that I am not like this Pharisee."[53]

Conceit, then, need not be obvious; it can be disguised as humility. According to Kierkegaard, this is one of Christian history's more disquieting lessons: "Christianity came into the world and taught

---

53. SKS 11, 263–64 / WA, 127.

humility, but not everyone learned humility from Christianity; hypocrisy learned how to change its mask and remain the same or, rather, become even worse."[54]

But this problem goes deeper than duplicity or pretense. As has been seen, faith is a kind of humility, and so without humility there is no faith. Hence, if sin has infiltrated and compromised Christian humility, faith too has been compromised. Herein lies an additional connection between "The Tax Collector" and *The Sickness unto Death*: whereas the latter details the nature of faith, the former pictures the humility essential to faith. In this way, "The Tax Collector" not only clarifies Anti-Climacus's teaching, but also constitutes another attempt to identify and to root out despair.

Kierkegaard accomplishes this task by attending to the tax collector himself. First, he notes that, unlike the Pharisee, the publican understands his relation to God is not defined by others. He does not use "other people to measure his distance from them."[55] Thus the tax collector avoids the dreaded vice of comparison and, in doing so, correctly understands that faith involves a willingness to be oneself before God. This point, Kierkegaard adds, puts the publican's spatial isolation—that he "stood off at a distance"—into proper perspective. These words do not allude to an aloofness from fellowship. Rather, the publican's separation represents the means by which one properly understands oneself and God. Alone, the tax collector recognizes his own "guilt and offense;"[56] he does not delude himself by measuring himself against other persons. Like Anti-Climacus, Kierkegaard insists that self-honesty, even if it is painful, is preferable to self-deception.

54. SKS 11, 264 / WA, 127.
55. SKS 11, 265 / WA, 129.
56. SKS 11, 265 / WA, 129.

Yet, the tax collector's faithful solitude is not only a matter of self-examination. It is also the condition for experiencing the majesty and holiness of God. Kierkegaard depicts the publican's unwillingness to look up to heaven as an encounter with the *mysterium tremendum*:

> *And he would not even lift up his eyes to heaven*; that is, he cast his eyes down. Well, no wonder! Even physically there is something in the infinite that overwhelms a person since there is nothing on which he can fix his eyes. This effect is called dizziness; then one must shut one's eyes. And the one who, alone with his guilt and his sin, knows that if he opens his eyes he will see God's holiness and nothing else, that one surely learns to cast his eyes down; or he perhaps looked up and saw God's holiness—and cast his eyes down.[57]

Stripped of pretense and rendered bare (transparent) before the Wholly Other, the publican can do nothing but call for God's help. According to Kierkegaard, this cry is an outcome of the tax collector's self-integration. Rid of the double-mindedness of despair, he now sees himself as he is and God as God is. Herein lies fear but also deliverance: "If only the danger and the terror are actual, the cry is always sincere, but, more than that, God be praised, it is not futile either."[58]

Indeed, the tax collector *"went home to his house justified."*[59] Kierkegaard points out that the publican stands as "the picture"[60] [*Billedet*] of justification, whereas the Pharisee is an image of condemnation. This result may seem surprising on a mundane level, since it is the tax collector who looks down, *away* from the heavens. However, he sees in and through faith, and "no look [*Blik*] is as sharp-sighted as that of faith . . ."[61] Faith is a kind of seeing, but it sees

57. SKS 11, 266 / WA, 130.
58. SKS 11, 267 / WA, 131.
59. SKS 11, 267 / WA, 131.
60. SKS 11, 268 / WA, 132.
61. SKS 11, 268 / WA, 132. The Hongs translate *Blik* as "gaze," but its simplest meaning is "look"—a word that better accords with Marion's insights. Thus I have changed it above.

through humility rather than strength: "[T]he downcast look [*Blik*] is sighted, and what the downcast look signifies is humility—humility is the uplifting."[62] In this way, Kierkegaard puts a fresh spin on the doctrine of "justification by faith." In his view, one is indeed justified by faith, but not just *any* faith. It is essential that faith be humble.[63]

In conclusion, Kierkegaard draws a comparison between the image of the tax collector and that of one participating in the Eucharist. Just as the publican stands off, effacing himself before God, so does the communicant "kneel at the Communion table, since to kneel is like a symbol of standing far off, far off from the one who is in heaven . . . and yet at the Communion table you are closest to God."[64] Here, then, is a collage of sorts. Kierkegaard uses different images to form a whole picture—a picture of faith's humility, which is the same today as it was yesterday. For "the person who truly learned to know God, and by learning to know God learned to know himself, finds blessedness only in falling upon his knees . . ."[65]

Faith as Suffering

In a 1998 essay, Klaus-M. Kodalle notes that, for Kierkegaard, suffering is always already a part of faith. In other words, one cannot have faith without suffering—a claim that Kodalle links to Kierkegaard's understanding of the relation between faith and reason. Whereas the latter is bound to the "instrumental rationality immanent in human society,"[66] the former involves the abandonment

62. SKS 11, 268 / WA, 132.
63. Precisely where this claim situates Kierkegaard vis-à-vis the Lutheran notion of "justification by faith alone" is an intriguing question, albeit one that outstrips the present discussion.
64. SKS 11, 269 / WA, 133.
65. SKS 11, 269 / WA, 134.
66. Klaus-M. Kodalle, "The Utilitarian Self and the 'Useless' Passion of Faith," in *The Cambridge Companion to Kierkegaard*, 398.

of just this use of reason. Faith, then, does not renounce reason as such. It renounces reason's attempts to master the world in order "to serve life's purposes."[67] Faith does not "get" a person anything. It is the death of what Kodalle calls the "utilitarian self," and, as with all deaths, "this movement means letting oneself in for 'unintelligible' suffering."[68]

Though he does not draw directly on *The Sickness unto Death*, Kodalle's analysis dovetails with that of Anti-Climacus, who treats faith as a way of being rather than as an acquisition. For Anti-Climacus, the spiritual journey from despair to faith involves the relinquishment of control. One has to forego the idea that *this* world alone is all there is and that it is there for the taking. Likewise, one has to give up the comfort of existing in fantastical categories, which bend to the self's will precisely insofar as they are detached from concrete existence. The self of faith synthesizes the finite and the infinite, and this integration entails an acceptance of bodily life with attention to the invisible source from which it has emerged. Thus faith's suffering is not tantamount to martyrdom.[69] Rather, it involves a willingness to *bear* with life as it is, whether in joy or in sorrow. Kierkegaard images this aspect of faith in his discourses on Job and Paul.

---

67. Ibid.
68. Ibid., 408.
69. However, it is implicit in martyrdom. The word "martyr" comes from the Greek *martyr*, and it literally means "witness." Of course, one can witness without suffering, but Christian history tends to celebrate those who have suffered for their witness. Attention to the word "suffering" clarifies this point. Taken from the Latin *sufferre*, to suffer is literally to bear up [*sub-ferre*] or to undergo something. The great martyrs of the Christian faith certainly have submitted to physical pain in order to testify to the gospel. But this physical pain is not essential. Rather, it is an accident stemming from a more basic suffering—namely, the conscious acceptance of their lives before God.

Job

In 1843, Kierkegaard issued three collections of upbuilding discourses. The third collection opens with a treatise on the biblical figure of Job. Entitled "The Lord Gave, and the Lord Took Away; Blessed Be the Name of the Lord," its task is to consider Job not only as a teacher but, above all, as a *Forbillede*—a term the Hongs translate as "prototype."[70]

This rendering, however, is less than ideal. A "prototype" is an original model on which later kinds are patterned, and, admittedly, Kierkegaard does use the term in this way. And yet, people tend to speak of "prototypes" of, say, cars or missiles, and in those cases the prototype establishes a pattern that is mechanically, even slavishly followed. But wherever Kierkegaard invokes a *Forbillede* he has something else in mind. A *Forbillede* is, to be precise, an image [*Billede*] that goes in front [*for*]. It is not a static picture but, rather, one to which a person is conformed according to her free and ongoing consent. "The Lord Gave" serves as an occasion for just this sort of conformity. In it one sees Job, an icon of faith, whose life serves "as a guide for everyone."[71]

Kierkegaard begins by noting that Job's famous saying, "[T]he Lord gave, and the Lord took away; blessed be the name of the Lord" (Job 1:21), cannot be understood apart from his life. In other words, it cannot be grasped *in abstracto*; one has to attend to Job himself, lest his words be received as a cliché. Moreover, one can only understand the saying to the degree that one "has been tried and who tested the saying in being tested himself . . ."[72] Job is a prototype who shines forth a wisdom that cannot be reduced to human concepts or bromides. It must be *encountered*.

70. SKS 5, 115 / EUD, 109.
71. SKS 5, 115 / EUD, 109.
72. SKS 5, 118 / EUD, 112.

This stress on the poverty of language is, according to Kierkegaard, implicit in the biblical account of Job's suffering. Upon learning of his great misfortune, Job does not "make use of many words, or rather he [does] not say a single one; his appearance alone [gives] witness . . ."[73] That Job speaks later does not contradict this point. His words merely articulate his visage—a visage that, according to the biblical account, expresses both Job's sorrow and his continued faith in God. "Then Job arose and tore his robe and shaved his head and fell on the ground and worshiped" (Job 1:20). Job countenances a kind of balance, exhibiting the concrete emotions of human grief, even as he discriminates between mutable earthly life and the eternal ways of God.[74]

This integration, as Kierkegaard goes on, makes up the substance of Job's faith. Job's refusal to succumb to his hardship—that is, to understand his life solely in relation to his earthly suffering—is expressed by his recognition that "[t]he LORD gave" (Job 1:21). In the face of such tragedy, these words may seem "irrelevant to the occasion."[75] Is this not a time to attend to life's heartbreak, to its ineluctable pain? But Job avoids the temptation to assess the situation unilaterally. He pushes despair away by retaining a view of the whole of existence: "[Job] recalled everything the Lord had given . . .; it had not become less beautiful because it had been taken away, nor more beautiful, but was just as beautiful as before, beautiful because the Lord had given it . . ."[76]

It is, as Kierkegaard adds, a delicate equipoise. Another person might recall the joy of times past, only to fall into an agonizing reverie. "What had been his eyes' delight, his eyes craved to see again, and his ingratitude punished him by inducing him to believe it to

73. SKS 5, 120 / EUD, 114.
74. SKS 5, 120 / EUD, 115.
75. SKS 5, 120 / EUD, 115.
76. SKS 5, 121 / EUD, 116.

be more beautiful than it had ever been."[77] Abandoned to "fantasies," such a person would be consumed by a "burning restlessness [*Uro*]."[78] Someone else, meanwhile, might choose "to waste his energies in impotent defiance,"[79] refusing to accept the loss in a desperate wish to take control of the situation. And yet another might desert any hope of being reconciled to the pain, choosing instead to plunge himself into the "abyss"[80] of forgetfulness. Each case is, as Kierkegaard reiterates, an example of *Uro*, and thus each stands in contrast to Job's equanimity [*Ro*]. For Job "remained what he was from the beginning," a man who "deceived neither God nor himself."[81] He wills to be himself before God.

It is at this point, however, that Kierkegaard anticipates a number of objections. Could not one counter that Job's faith is illusory, since it traces his misfortune back to God rather than attending to the mundane causes of his suffering? Does not Job exemplify a deplorable sort of religiousness, which seeks comfort in metaphysical speculations while ignoring the very real problems of earthly life—the wars, natural disasters, and murders? Moreover, does not Job do a disservice to God himself, asserting that "the LORD has taken away" (Job 1:21) when true piety would clear God of such heinous charges?

Kierkegaard assumes that, from a certain perspective, these are legitimate questions. What he distrusts is their effect on the self. The ascription of human suffering to mere chance engenders confusion, while stressing "the deceit and cunning of people"[82] begets misanthropy. Likewise, focusing on natural disasters brings a certain "horror," for it exposes the fragility and contingency of life on

77. SKS 5, 122 / EUD, 117.
78. SKS 5, 122 / EUD, 117.
79. SKS 5, 123 / EUD, 118.
80. SKS 5, 123 / EUD, 118.
81. SKS 5, 123 / EUD, 118.
82. SKS 5, 124 / EUD, 119.

earth—a place where "mountains sigh [and] men and their glorious works . . . sink as a nothingness into the abyss."[83] But worst of all is blaming oneself, which leads one to self-doubt and to an endless run of questions which make it "impossible . . . to learn anything from life . . ."[84]

It is worth noting that this is an issue that crops up elsewhere in Kierkegaard's authorship. The final section of *Either/Or* is a pseudonymous sermon, "The Upbuilding that Lies in the Thought that in Relation to God We are Always in the Wrong." It contends that, although human beings are either more or less upright in their relations with one another, this sort of comparison does not obtain with God, who is the origin and end of earthly existence. Consequently, one must avoid the temptation to determine where one stands with God—an effort that both misunderstands the divine nature and locks the self in a cycle of despair. It would be far better to submit to the eternal, asking for forgiveness and mercy and, in turn, receiving upbuilding.

In a later work, *Stages on Life's Way*, Kierkegaard painstakingly (and, often for the reader, painfully) demonstrates what happens when a person fails to adopt this spiritual approach. The author of the book's diary-like portion, "Guilty?—Not Guilty?", stands at a crossroads. Lamenting a failed relationship, "he could go in a specifically religious direction by choosing to see himself as guilty, without further calculation, or he could use the process of deliberation about guilt as a way of procrastinating and avoiding repentance . . ."[85] As the diary slogs on, it becomes evident that the latter is the case. Immobilized by "infinite reflection,"[86] the writer

83. SKS 5, 125 / EUD, 120.
84. SKS 5, 125 / EUD, 120.
85. Watkin, *Kierkegaard's Philosophy*, 406–07.
86. SKS 6, 382 / SLW, 413.

drifts into a kind of nihilism, unmoored from God and from the world, indifferent to everything but his own despair.

Alas, Kierkegaard suggests, human suffering always presents such a danger. The wonder of faith is that it is able to sublimate suffering into something higher. Job images this sublimation:

> Job traced everything back to God; he did not detain his soul and quench his spirit with deliberation or explanations that only feed and foster doubt, even though the person suspended in them does not even notice that. The very moment everything was taken away from him, he knew it was the Lord who had taken it away, and therefore in his loss he remained on good terms with the Lord, in his loss maintained intimacy with the Lord; he saw the Lord, and therefore he did not see despair.[87]

The question, in other words, is not *whether* a human being will suffer, but *how* he or she will suffer. Job represents faith's suffering, which submits to God but, for just that reason, "has overcome the world."[88]

Kierkegaard concludes by recalling that Job's great saying ends with words of benediction: "[B]lessed be the name of the LORD" (Job 1:21). This is a sign of "the bold confidence of faith,"[89] which in sorrow redoubles its strength precisely by recognizing that, when all else has fallen away, God remains. Frequently, this fact is neglected amid the busyness of life. However, suffering brings it to the forefront, deepening one's friendship with God because now nothing is "capable of drawing [one's] thoughts away."[90]

Thus Job stands as the "image of sorrow"[91] transfigured into blessing. That is why his example is particularly meaningful to those

87. SKS 5, 125 / EUD, 121.
88. SKS 5, 125 / EUD, 121.
89. SKS 5, 126 / EUD, 122.
90. SKS 5, 126 / EUD, 122.
91. SKS 5, 126 / EUD, 122.

who suffer, even though, Kierkegaard is quick to add, all must eventually confront his iconic figuring of faith:

> [A]re you perhaps thinking that something like this could not happen to you? Who taught you this wisdom, or on what do you base this conviction? Are you wise and sensible, and is this your comfort? Job was the teacher of many people. Are you young, and is youth your security? Job, too, was once young. Are you old, on the edge of the grave? Job was an old man when sorrow caught up with him. Are you powerful, and is this the proof of your exemption? Job was highly regarded by the people. Is wealth your security? Job possessed the blessings of the land. Are your friends your security? Job was loved by all. Do you trust in God? Job was an intimate of the Lord.[92]

In short, everyone must admit that "there is no hiding place in the whole wide world where trouble will not find you . . ."[93] In this scenario, one either can pretend otherwise, or one can contemplate Job. Kierkegaard's recommendation is no surprise: "[B]e earnest with yourself; fix your eyes upon Job."[94]

Paul

For Kierkegaard, faith always already implies suffering, since, in faith, one comes to bear with one's life as it is, resting in the will of the one who established it. Job symbolizes this aspect of faith. He refers his earthly sorrows back to God and, in doing so, exemplifies faith's transmutation of suffering into joy.

But what if the opposite were to take place? What if joy were transmuted into suffering, spiritual bliss into spiritual torment? Could faith bear with *that* change too? Kierkegaard addresses these questions

92. SKS 5, 128 / EUD, 123–24.
93. SKS 5, 128 / EUD, 124.
94. SKS 5, 128 / EUD, 124.

in "The Thorn in the Flesh," the second piece of 1844's *Four Upbuilding Discourses*.

As with "The Lord Gave, and the Lord Took Away; Blessed Be the Name of the Lord," "The Thorn in the Flesh" takes its cue from a celebrated biblical passage—in this case, the words of the Apostle Paul:

> I refrain from [boasting], so that no one may think better of me than what is seen in me or heard from me, even considering the exceptional character of the revelations. Therefore, to keep me from being too elated, a thorn was given me in the flesh, a messenger of Satan to torment me, to keep me from being too elated (2 Cor. 12:6-7).

Kierkegaard observes that, as with other great scriptural maxims, Paul's words about a "thorn in the flesh" have been rendered platitudinous. Even worse, they have been expounded and picked apart by biblical exegetes, whose "ingenuity"[95] has made the text conformable to all manner of situations, no matter how absurd or banal. But Paul's saying is not like that: it does not concern everyday nuisances but, rather, speaks to a "crucial struggle"—namely, the "distress of spiritual trial."[96]

The concept of "spiritual trial" [*Anfægtelse*] extends well beyond Kierkegaard's authorship. Related to the German term *Anfechtung*, often translated as "temptation," it literally means "being fought against." As Daphne Hampson puts it, "*Anfechtung* . . . is the word used within the Lutheran tradition for the sense that one is undermined/caught/pinned down when confronted by God."[97] Thus *Anfechtung* is not "temptation" in the typical sense of the word, signifying an attraction to some voluptuous pleasure (food, sex, and

---

95. SKS 5, 319 / EUD, 328.
96. SKS 5, 320–21 / EUD, 330–31.
97. Daphne Hampson, *Christian Contradictions: The Structures of Lutheran and Catholic Thought* (Cambridge: Cambridge University Press, 2001), 256.

the like) against the divine will. On the contrary, it is an oppressive sense of one's fallenness and impotence before heaven and earth.[98] Simon Podmore notes that, for Martin Luther, *Anfechtung* also stems from a peculiar arrangement between God and Satan: "God implicitly grants to the devil power over human beings," particularly to "afflict the faithful."[99] But Kierkegaard departs from this perspective, deeming it "more childish than true."[100] He prefers to "situate the tension of spiritual trial irreducibly between the individual and God,"[101] even though, with Luther, he agrees that spiritual trial is most likely to affect the person of faith.[102] In short, Kierkegaard equates *Anfægtelse* with the self's struggle to "immediately and completely surrender to God."[103]

"The Thorn in the Flesh" not only corroborates this point, but seeks to embody it in the figure of Paul himself. Indeed, Paul makes the ideal subject, because he was accustomed to so many different types of suffering. He was "derided as mentally disordered," imprisoned, abused, "abandoned by friends," "forgotten," even "regarded as a seducer."[104] But none of these sufferings, Kierkegaard adds, are *Anfægtelse*, the suffering of faith. The difference lies in one's internal state. When the external world presses in on the faithful person, there remains "assurance that he is in harmony with God."[105] Paul expresses this harmony by speaking of being caught up into the third heaven.[106] And yet, it is precisely here, at the apex of spiritual

---

98. Simon D. Podmore, *Kierkegaard and the Self Before God* (Bloomington: Indiana University Press, 2011), 122.
99. Ibid., 128.
100. SKS 21, NB9:22 / JP 4, 4372.
101. Podmore, *Kierkegaard and the Self Before God*, 129.
102. SKS 21, NB9:22 / JP 4, 4372.
103. SKS 26, NB33:54 / JP 4, 4384.
104. SKS 5, 322 / EUD, 333.
105. SKS 5, 322–23 / EUD, 333.
106. 2 Cor. 2:12. Cf. SKS 5, 323 / EUD, 334.

ecstasy, that the thorn in the flesh festers. Spiritual trial is but the flipside of spiritual beatitude. They "correspond to each other."[107]

Hence, although Paul is known as the great champion of faith, his thorn in the flesh also discloses one of faith's most profound mysteries—that its joy is never pure, that its bliss is ever fleeting. Over against all manner of earthly sufferings, the person of faith might come to believe that *control* has finally been attained, since neither the epithets of oppressors nor the pain of disease are capable of disturbing her. But the thorn in the flesh punctures such hopes and, in doing so, reminds one that faith entails the very abyss of "powerlessness."[108] Kierkegaard again invokes the figure of Paul:

> To have been caught up into the third heaven, to have been hidden in the bosom of beatitude, to have been expanded in God, and now to be tethered by the thorn in the flesh to the thralldom of temporality! To have been made rich in God, inexpressibly so, and now to be broken down to flesh and blood, to dust and corruption![109]

This is, according to Kierkegaard, a kind of spiritual imprisonment: Paul had experienced the eternal and its consolations of forgiveness and love, only to be thrust back into the "fragile earthen vessel"[110] of temporal life. What's more, he now realized that solace really does not come in this world and that one "can aspire to it only in faith."[111]

Implicit in Kierkegaard's point here is that faith always involves a desire to start over, to turn around. No one exemplifies this wish better than Paul, whose conversion to Christianity occasioned a new name, not to mention a new way of life. And yet, says Kierkegaard, "there was nevertheless a memory."[112] Paul must have remembered

---

107. SKS 5, 324 / EUD, 335.
108. SKS 5, 325 / EUD, 337.
109. SKS 5, 325 / EUD, 337.
110. SKS 5, 326 / EUD, 337.
111. SKS 5, 328 / EUD, 339.
112. SKS 5, 329 / EUD, 341.

his past life—his persecution of Christians, his misunderstanding of God's will, his manifold failures.[113] Surely, these anxieties wounded Paul's confidence and cast doubt on his conversion. But he learned they could be overcome only by suffering. He had to rest *in* them, rather than fight *against* them. In this way, faith turns the angel of Satan into "an emissary of God."[114]

Even so, the thorn in the flesh will never be totally removed in this life. "There is no security in time,"[115] as Kierkegaard states. This is part of the "terror"[116] of the upbuilding. No matter how hard one tries to change one's life, no matter how deeply one's past seems to be buried, there is always the possibility of "relapse" or, at the very least, "anxiety about the relapse."[117] As an icon of faith, Paul represents the way forward. He "understands that this is beneficial for him, that . . . every self-confidence that wants to be finished must be burned out in the purgatory of the future, every cowardliness that wants to sneak past the danger must perish in the desert of expectancy."[118] In both the beatitude of heaven *and* the earthly thorn in the flesh, Paul places his trust in God. He realizes that peace "depends not on human will or exertion, but on God, who has mercy."[119]

Kierkegaard's conclusion to "The Thorn in the Flesh" serves as a fitting end to this section. He reiterates that suffering is an essential, rather than an accidental, aspect of faith. In other words, it is not a misfortune that *happens* to the person of faith but a feature that *follows* from faith's very nature: "the highest life . . . has the hardest suffering."[120] This point is crucial, lest faith be confused with a

113. SKS 5, 329–30 / EUD, 341–42.
114. SKS 5, 330 / EUD, 342.
115. SKS 5, 331 / EUD, 343.
116. SKS 5, 331 / EUD, 344.
117. SKS 5, 332 / EUD, 345.
118. SKS 5, 333 / EUD, 345.
119. Rom. 9:16. Cf. SKS 5, 333 / EUD, 345.
120. SKS 5, 334 / EUD, 346.

utopian egress from life's pain and sorrow. Of course, no one who attends to Kierkegaard's icons of Job and Paul would make that mistake, nor, on the other hand, would they forget that the one who faces suffering "is already on the way to begin the good fight."[121] The key, for Kierkegaard, is to seek the good in all things, to rest in God—yes, to refer everything back to God, *even* one's failure to rest in God. Then the "comfort will surely come."[122]

Faith as Love

To this point, it has been shown that faith involves two different aspects. First, it is humble. The one who has faith places oneself neither above others nor above God. Second, it is patient. The one who has faith neither seeks flight from suffering nor reduces earthly life to a *valle lacrimarum*. Both of these aspects correspond to Kierkegaard's insistence that faith be understood as rest—indeed, not only as rest in God, but also as rest in who one is and in who one wants to be.

The relation between faith and love, however, is less straightforward. Despite Kierkegaard's emphasis on the importance of faith, he nevertheless situates *love* at the heart of Christianity. As he puts it in an early journal entry, love is the *"primus motor"*[123] of the Christian life. Moreover, in arguably his most famous set of discourses, *Works of Love* (1847), he states that "[t]o defraud oneself of love is the most terrible, is an eternal loss, for which there is no compensation either in time or in eternity."[124] In so elevating love, Kierkegaard might be seen as diminishing the centrality of

---

121. SKS 5, 334 / EUD, 346.
122. SKS 5, 334 / EUD, 346.
123. SKS 18, 14, EE:25 / JP 3, 2383.
124. SKS 9, 14 / WL, 6.

faith. His words call to mind the viewpoint of the Apostle Paul, whose famed encomium on love states that, in relation to other Christian virtues, "the greatest of these is love" (1 Cor. 13:13). Yet, this similarity leads to a few key questions. Do Kierkegaard's views on love supersede or even contradict the stress on faith found elsewhere in his authorship? Was Anti-Climacus mistaken when he insisted that the opposite of sin is faith, rather than virtue or love?[125] *In nuce*, how does Kierkegaard correlate faith and love?

Kierkegaard's journals show that he wrestled with this question for some time. Already in 1834 a pair of journal entries question the link between faith and volitional activity.[126] Then, in 1836, Kierkegaard hits on an understanding that will come to characterize his analysis of the problem. Comparing faith to a "vital fluid" and to "the atmosphere we breathe," he concludes that it is "the prerequisite for everything."[127] He later reworks this notion, explaining that faith is the "a priori" that "hovers over all the a posteriori of works."[128] Intriguingly, Kierkegaard likens this position to that of Paul[129]—a point borne out by scholarship on the apostle's epistles. According to J. Paul Sampley, Paul understands faith as "the right relation to God," which, in turn, "makes love possible."[130] In other words, "love presupposes faith."[131] But this perspective does not place faith *over* love. Faith is a "human commitment" that "may end," whereas love, "grounded as it is in God and a signal and eternal characteristic of God's commitment toward all creatures, is the one disposition that believers share most fully with God."[132] Thus love flows from faith

---

125. SKS 11, 196 / SUD, 82.
126. SKS, 27, 97, Papir 58 / JP 2, 1094; SKS, 27, 99, Papir 62 / JP 2, 1095.
127. SKS 27, 112, Papir 92 / JP 2, 1096.
128. SKS 17, 247, DD:79 / JP 2, 1097.
129. See, e.g., Rom. 8:35-39.
130. J. Paul Sampley, "The First Letter to the Corinthians," in *The New Interpreter's Bible*, ed. Leander E. Keck et al. (Nashville: Abingdon, 2002), 10:955.
131. Ibid.
132. Ibid.

and, indeed, is its perfection. But without faith it could not begin. To return to Kierkegaard's language, faith is the prerequisite for everything.

Kierkegaard develops this line of reasoning at the outset of *Works of Love*. He opens with a prayer, which lauds the "God of love."[133] Here the term he uses for "love" is *Kjerlighed*, which can be compared to the Latin term *caritas*, signifying non-erotic benevolence or kindness.[134] Thus God is *Kjerlighed*. Kierkegaard presents this point in Trinitarian fashion, describing God as "the source of all love in heaven and on earth,"[135] "the Savior and Redeemer," "who revealed what love is," and the "Spirit of love," who reminds "the believer to love as he is loved and his neighbor as himself . . ."[136] In emphasizing love's divine origin, Kierkegaard is also stressing its mystery. As M. Jamie Ferreira puts it, "[L]ove is hidden because its source is God, who is hidden, who is invisible, a 'secret source.'"[137] The same is true for *Kjerlighed* in human life, which, stemming from God, "dwells in hiding or is hidden in the innermost being."[138] In turn, *Kjerlighed* does not proceed from a calculus of cost-benefit. It is not like a coin, which is presented in exchange for something else. Rather, it is given, even without recognition, for the sake of the beloved.

---

133. SKS 9, 12 / WL, 3.
134. For that reason, *Kjerlighed* is often contrasted with its Danish counterpart, *Elskov*, which indicates erotic or sensual love. That does not mean, however, that the two are mutually exclusive. For Kierkegaard, in particular, *Kjerlighed* might be seen as the completion of *Elskov*, since, without *Kjerlighed*, *Elskov* cannot be sustained in nonviolent fashion. As he explains, Christianity "has made erotic love a matter of conscience," since it refuses to reduce love to "drives and inclination" (SKS 9, 142 / WL, 140). Put simply, Christianity also treats the erotic lover as "the neighbor," whom one is supposed to love as oneself. In this way, the Christian stress on *Kjerlighed*, which reflects a participation in the nature of God, protects "what was begun on the basis of the erotic" (Watkin, *Kierkegaard's Philosophy*, 155).
135. SKS 9, 12 / WL, 3.
136. SKS 9, 12 / WL, 3–4.
137. M. Jamie Ferreira, *Love's Grateful Striving: A Commentary on Kierkegaard's* Works of Love (Oxford: Oxford University Press, 2001), 22.
138. SKS 9, 17 / WL, 9.

Yet, precisely because this sort of love confounds ordinary ways of doing things, precisely because its saturation of the created order renders it incomprehensible, one must have *faith* in it. One must believe it is there. The first discourse of *Works of Love*, "Love's Hidden Life and its Recognizability by its Fruits," emphasizes this point. The tendency of "conceited sagacity," he begins, is to "believe nothing that we cannot see with our physical eyes."[139] But this way of thinking carries a decisive implication: "we first and foremost ought to give up believing in love,"[140] which cannot be empirically demonstrated. Such logic, says Kierkegaard, ought to give one pause for thought. It is true that no one in life wants to be "deceived by believing what is untrue."[141] And yet, this impulse can be taken too far. One can become obsessed with wanting to make oneself "absolutely secure against being deceived,"[142] policing out anything that lacks experimental proof. But this is itself a deception—indeed, a more intractable and damaging deception. For such a person, proud of his or her intelligence, is "deceived by not believing what is true."[143]

The challenge, then, is to have faith in love. It is to believe that love is present, not only in human life, but also in eternity. In fact, these two loves go hand in hand:

> [Love] is in an unfathomable connectedness with all existence. Just as the quiet lake originates deep down in hidden springs no eye has seen, so also does a person's love [*Kjerlighed*] originate even more deeply in God's love [*Kjerlighed*]. If there were no gushing spring at the bottom, if God were not love, then there would be neither the little lake nor a human being love.[144]

139. SKS 9, 13 / WL, 5.
140. SKS 9, 13 / WL, 5.
141. SKS 9, 13 / WL, 5.
142. SKS 9, 13 / WL, 5.
143. SKS 9, 13 / WL, 5.
144. SKS 9, 17–18 / WL, 9–10.

Seen without faith, viewed from the inclosing perspective of worldliness, this icon becomes an idol. "When you think that you see [love's essence], you are deceived by a reflected image."[145] That is why faith is necessary. It does not seek to infiltrate the mystery of love but, rather, to presuppose it, to rest in its presence.[146] In this way, faith is like a channel, which allows one to "tune in" to the reality of love. Faith does not create love but enables the human being to cooperate with it—a point that brings this discussion full-circle. For Kierkegaard, as for Paul, love and its works are the perfection of faith. Yet, it is also true that love is an aspect of faith, since, without faith, love could not be perceived in the world.

With this point established, it is now time to turn to the icons of faith's love in Kierkegaard's authorship. Two such icons will be considered, Jesus Christ and the woman who was a sinner. Kierkegaard's treatment of Christ as an icon will be discussed first, as Christ's total rest in the Father and in the Spirit signifies the *ne plus ultra* of faith and, with it, of love. In this way, Christ is the highest *Forbillede*, the perfect icon of faith, whose example both inspires and shocks—a point that Kierkegaard repeatedly stresses, especially in his later authorship.

Here, again, faith is needed to see Christ correctly. Yet, when this faith is present, it transforms the person, grounding him in God and so in love. Kierkegaard images this sort of faith in his discourses on the woman who was a sinner, whom he explicitly calls a picture of godliness. As will be seen, her image paradoxically comes to resemble that of Christ. Her faith finds expression in the love of Love itself. Christ may be the highest *Forbillede*, but, Kierkegaard suggests, fallen human beings ought not strain to reach his example. Like this

---

145. SKS 9, 18 / WL, 10.
146. Kierkegaard develops this insight poignantly later in *Works of Love*, namely, in the discourse "Love Hides a Multitude of Sins."

formerly sinful woman, they only need to recline at Christ's feet, for in this rest lies renewal and the very possibility of Christlikeness. Thus the woman who was a sinner marks a fitting conclusion to this chapter and, in turn, to this book.

Jesus Christ

That Kierkegaard pays a great deal of attention to Jesus Christ has long been noticed. One commentator has even deemed his theology "Christocentric."[147] Moreover, Christology is an area of Kierkegaard's thought that lends itself to systematic analysis, as evinced by texts on Kierkegaard's conception of *imitatio Christi*,[148] on his understanding of conversion to Christ,[149] and on the kenotic elements of his Christology[150]—just to name a few. What follows, however, is not a methodical examination of Kierkegaard's Christology. The goal, rather, is to survey Kierkegaard's stress on the *image* of Christ and on the importance of contemplating it.[151]

The figure of Christ turns up in various modes throughout Kierkegaard's authorship. Below two features will receive particular consideration, namely, Kierkegaard's emphases on Christ as "sign" [*Tegn*] and on Christ as "prototype" [*Forbillede*]. As will be seen, these pictorial approaches are not mutually exclusive. In fact, there is a very real sense in which the former points to the latter. The one who views

147. Timothy Rose, *Kierkegaard's Christocentric Theology* (Aldershot: Ashgate, 2001).

148. Bradley R. Dewey, *The New Obedience: Kierkegaard on Imitating Christ* (Washington, DC: Corpus Books, 1968). Also see Christopher B. Barnett, *Kierkegaard, Pietism and Holiness* (Farnham: Ashgate, 2011), especially Chapter Six.

149. Murray Rae, *Kierkegaard's Vision of the Incarnation: By Faith Transformed* (Oxford: Clarendon, 1997).

150. David R. Law, *Kierkegaard's Kenotic Christology* (Oxford: Oxford University Press, 2013).

151. Of course, that is not to say that this section has no relation to systematic Christological and theological questions. However, the interests of this particular study require that these problems be set in the background.

the "sign" of Christ in faith is, accordingly, moved to follow Christ's example of faith and love.

First, however, it is worth reflecting on the significance that Christ's image had in Kierkegaard's own life. To be sure, growing up in a Pietist household, Kierkegaard would have encountered "pictures" of Christ from a young age. As mentioned in Chapter Three, Kierkegaard was familiar with the Moravian practice of contemplating the crucified Christ, not just in hymnody and prayer, but also in imagery—a tendency exemplified in the works of the great Moravian painter, Johann Valentin Haidt, who "came to consider . . . painting as a means of 'testifying to his Savior's death and passion.'"[152] For the Moravians, Christian faith is always already more than a cognitive assent to doctrines regarding Christ's salvific work. It is a mysterious encounter with Christ himself, often mediated through images, sounds, and so on.

That Kierkegaard was raised on this approach is indicated in his writings, albeit in somewhat oblique fashion. His 1849 essay, "Does a Human Being Have the Right to Let Himself Be Put to Death for the Truth?," attributed to the pseudonym, H. H., begins with a lengthy passage about a man who "had been strictly brought up in the Christian religion."[153] From a young age this man had been taught to ponder the "picture" [*Billede*] of the crucified Christ, so much so that as he got older he "could not for one moment look away from this picture that drew him to itself."[154] Slowly but surely "the picture . . . came closer and closer to him, and he felt its claim on him ever more deeply."[155] Here H. H. gets at the very heart of what an icon is: it is not a static image but a dynamic medium, which redirects

---

152. Garth A. Howland, "John Valentine Haidt: A Little Known Eighteenth Century Painter," *Pennsylvania History* 8, no. 4 (1941): 304.
153. SKS 11, 61 / WA, 55.
154. SKS 11, 61 / WA, 55.
155. SKS 11, 62 / WA, 55–56.

the observer's vision to the transcendent. Indeed, in this case, the man refuses "to look artistically at such a painted picture,"[156] since the *Billede* is not an end in itself. Its purpose is to reorient the one looking at it. For that reason, the man is at once drawn to and daunted by Christ's image: he wants to be changed, "to become like [the picture itself],"[157] but to what degree? Should he too be crucified?

It is a weighty introduction to the essay, which almost certainly bears autobiographical undertones. As Joakim Garff writes, "Somber images of [the crucified Christ] from the Moravian Congregation seized hold of [Kierkegaard's] imagination quite early and set their stamp on his view of life."[158] Nevertheless, the decisive aspect of H. H.'s story is not a macabre preoccupation with pain and suffering, but a stress on the ambiguity of Christ's image. One can look at it for years, H. H. implies, and still struggle to comprehend what it means. His treatise itself is an attempt to ponder the significance of Christ's likeness and, hopefully, to come to see it the right way. Only then will its true meaning be disclosed.

Writing as Anti-Climacus, Kierkegaard returns to this line of thinking in *Practice in Christianity*, but now with greater precision. According to Anti-Climacus, encountering Christ "is like standing at the crossroad."[159] One is either offended by Christ—whether due to his challenge to the powers-that-be, his lowly social status, or his shocking claims to divinity—or one has faith in him. This notion of "offense" is essentially synonymous with what Anti-Climacus calls "despair" in *The Sickness unto Death*.[160] For to be offended by Christ is to be offended by the harmonious coincidence of finitude and infinity, of eternality and temporality. In other words, offense at

---

156. SKS 11, 61 / WA, 55.
157. SKS 11, 62 / WA, 57.
158. Garff, *Kierkegaard*, 12.
159. SKS 12, 91 / PC, 81.
160. SKS 12, 91 / PC, 81.

Christ entails the refusal of faith itself, since Christ stands as the supreme embodiment of Anti-Climacan faith—a human nature transparently at rest, perfectly united, with its divine source.

For that reason, says Anti-Climacus, Christ is a *sign*. Here the Danish word *Tegn* recalls the English "token." Just as a token is at once an object (a circular piece of metal) and a signifier of something else (monetary value), so does Christ confront persons with a meaning (his divinity) beyond what he immediately appears to be (an ordinary human being). To call Christ a sign, then, is to say he provokes "reflection."[161] One has to contemplate who he is and what sort of value he has. Moreover, he is a "sign of contradiction,"[162] since, as the God-man, there is a "contradiction in [his] composition."[163] In this case, "contradiction" does not mean "ontological impossibility" but "logical incongruity." The former would not be worth dwelling on at all; it would be sheer ludicrousness. The latter, however, "draws attention to itself and then it presents a contradiction."[164] Christ communicates something remarkable, say, a miracle or the claim that he is divine. The person looking stops, contemplates. The image before her cannot be directly understood or appropriated. It confounds the facile significance of the idol—for "[d]irect recognizability is specifically characteristic of the idol"[165]—and opens up the complex, unsetting space of the icon. As Anti-Climacus puts it, "[Christ] who is the sign of contradiction looks straight into one's heart while one is staring into the contradiction."[166] Christ's countenance "discloses the thoughts of hearts."[167]

161. SKS 12, 129 / PC, 124.
162. SKS 12, 129 / PC, 124.
163. SKS 12, 130 / PC, 124–25.
164. SKS 12, 131 / PC, 126.
165. SKS 12, 139 / PC, 136.
166. SKS 12, 131 / PC, 127.
167. SKS 12, 131 / PC, 126.

Thus Christ not only personifies faith, but he necessitates the decision between offense and faith. If he could be known otherwise, he would be an idol, reduced to the immanent gaze of the human. "[I]f he does not become the object of *faith*, he is not true God . . ."[168] In contrast, faith always already presupposes the free cooperation of the human being. "Faith is a choice,"[169] which is tantamount to the human being's self-conscious willingness to rest in himself and in God. Unlike the answer to an algebraic equation, faith cannot be compelled. In fact, Christ's entire earthly comportment ensures that it is *not* compelled:

> The true God cannot become directly recognizable, but direct recognizability is what the purely human, what the human beings to whom he came, would plead and implore him for as an indescribable alleviation. And out of love he becomes man! He is love, and yet at every moment he exists he must crucify, so to speak, all human compassion and solicitude—for he can become only the object of faith.[170]

This passage uncannily anticipates Fyodor Dostoevsky's famous parable of "The Grand Inquisitor."[171] For Anti-Climacus, as for his Russian counterpart, Christ exemplifies the very burden of love. Faith comes from and tends toward love—this is the good news—but in between it involves a slow, painstaking detachment from deep-seated habits and predilections. Christ himself images this detachment but, at the same time, also offers it to his followers. Here the beauty and the terror of Christian existence converge.

Memorably, Anti-Climacus illustrates this point later in *Practice in Christianity*. "Picture to yourself this abased one,"[172] he begins. "What

---

168. SKS 12, 141 / PC, 137.
169. SKS 12, 144 / PC, 141.
170. SKS 12, 141 / PC, 137.
171. See Fyodor Dostoevsky, *The Brothers Karamazov*, trans. Richard Pevear and Larissa Volokhonsky (New York: Knopf, 1992), 246–64.
172. SKS 12, 173 / PC, 170.

effect does this sight [*Syn*] produce?"[173] He then calls to mind a "child who for the first time hears the story"[174] of Christ. This child, he imagines, is presented with "many pictures" [*Billeder*] of renowned figures—Napoleon first and then William Tell. He is delighted by these images, marveling at the grandeur and the bravery of the heroes. And then he sees a *Billede* of the crucified Christ. "The child will feel uncomfortable; he will probably wonder how it could occur to you to put such an ugly picture among all the other lovely pictures."[175] It is then explained that this figure, murdered in the manner of criminal, was "the Savior of the world," "the most loving person who ever lived,"[176] "who lived for only one thing—to love and to help people, especially all those who were sick and sorrowful and suffering and unhappy."[177] The child is stunned. How could such a thing happen? *Why* did it happen? The more he considers the image, the "more and more passionate"[178] he becomes, as if drawn into the sign's meaning. In time, and with due attention, he would come to see what Christian doctrine has long proclaimed—that "not only the person who, humanly speaking, wills the good must suffer, but that . . . there usually is living at the same time the despicable, the contemptible, the dastardly, who in contrast are applauded and cheered."[179] It is a frightful insight, yet one that, viewed with the eyes of faith, comes to love the profundity of Christ's love.[180] Indeed, it is this "sight that so moved the glorious ones whom the Church

---

173. SKS 12, 176 / PC, 174. Here the Danish word *Syn* could also be rendered as "vision" or "spectacle." Either way, there is a marked stress on Christ as an *icon*.
174. SKS 12, 176 / PC, 174.
175. SKS 12, 177 / PC, 175.
176. SKS 12, 177–78 / PC, 175.
177. SKS 12, 178 / PC, 176.
178. SKS 12, 179 / PC, 177.
179. SKS 12, 180 / PC, 178.
180. SKS 12, 180 / PC, 178. Anti-Climacus does not use the word "faith" here. Rather, he states, "[O]nly the person who loves him understands that he was love . . ." (SKS 12, 180 / PC, 178). Yet, as has been seen, Kierkegaard himself makes clear that one must *believe* in love in order to see it. Thus "faith" is implicit in Anti-Climacus's analysis.

remembers as its fathers and teachers,"[181] encouraging them "to want to suffer in a way akin to the suffering of [Christ]."[182] From Christ as sign one is brought to Christ as prototype.

George Pattison has remarked that this story exemplifies Kierkegaard's ability to use "visual representation" as a means of enabling "us to discover what it is for Christ to be proclaimed as pattern."[183] Still, he remains dubious that art can be enlisted in Kierkegaard's authorial project: "For the artist the crucifixion is simply an image, an object of contemplation, of detached appraisal . . ."[184] In traditional iconography, however, the contemplation of icons is not at all like "detached appraisal." These are different modes of seeing, requiring different mental and spiritual attitudes. In contemplation, one must come to the image with a sense of openness, trusting that "the limits of the visual image are [not] the limits of communication . . ."[185] Doubtless that is why Anti-Climacus's parable features a child, whose innocence exposes him to the terrifying but redemptive meaning of Calvary. The child is not saddled with the baggage of the adult; he does not despair over the image's historicity, artistic quality, or philosophical significance. He receives the image in the simplicity that Anti-Climacus calls "faith." The child lets the image move him.[186]

Once again, then, the *Tegn* of Christ points the way to Christ as *Forbillede*. Christ signifies faith's highest possibility—a human nature so at one with the divine that it reduplicates the divine nature itself, which is love—but this signification, as an icon, is also an ecstatic call.

181. SKS 12, 180 / PC, 178.
182. SKS 12, 180 / PC, 178.
183. George Pattison, *Kierkegaard: The Aesthetic and the Religious: From the Magic Theatre to the Crucifixion of the Image* (New York: St. Martin's, 1992), 185.
184. Ibid., 184.
185. Ibid., 188.
186. Of course, this approach has biblical warrant, as Jesus himself stresses the need to respond to the kingdom of God in the manner of a child. See, for example, Mark 10:13-16 and Luke 18:5-17.

Here "ecstatic" is intended in the sense of its Greek root [*ek histanai*], meaning "to displace" or "to draw out." When the *Tegn* of Christ is seen in faith, it draws one out of oneself and sets one on the path of love, which can never be circumscribed from the human side. The sign has become an "image that goes in front" [*Forbillede*], leading one to an unfathomable participation in love's way in the world.

Practice in Christianity itself features this transition from *Tegn* to *Forbillede*. The book's second part, as has been discussed, concerns the choice between faith and offense occasioned by the sign of Christ. Meanwhile, its third and final part, entitled "From on High He Will Draw All to Himself," consists of a series of "Christian Expositions" that stress how a "Christian's life is properly . . . oriented toward what is above, toward loftiness, toward him who on high draws the Christian to himself . . ."[187] This ascending movement involves a detachment from matters both sacred and profane: "there is much that must be forgotten, much that must be disregarded, much that must be died to."[188] And yet, as Anti-Climacus goes on, detachment itself can become a kind of fixation, which can lock the self within its own cares and concerns. Thus one must always keep Christ before the eyes of the mind.[189] And, in doing so, one's life will be drawn ever deeper into Christ's life, into a love so deep that it extends even to one's enemies, regardless of whether or not it will be reciprocated:

> If [the] Christian did not have the prototype to look at, he would not persevere, he would not dare to believe there was any love within himself when people testify against him. . . . But the prototype, who eternally knew in himself that he was love, whom therefore no world, not the whole world, could shake in this certainty, has expressly manifested that love is hated, truth is persecuted. Because of this image

187. SKS 12, 156 / PC, 152.
188. SKS 12, 156 / PC, 152.
189. SKS 12, 156 / PC, 152–53.

before his eyes, the Christian perseveres in abasement, drawn to him who from on high will draw all to himself.[190]

For Anti-Climacus, faith and love meet in the *imitatio Christi*.[191] To imitate Christ's lowly earthly life is a venture of faith—a faith that Christ, the incarnation of love, expresses what is really and finally real. At the same time, this belief will be challenged both from within and from without, thereby underscoring faith's humility and passion. The looming possibility of despair, so multifaceted on Anti-Climacus's reading, is a reminder of the need for divine consolation and encouragement. One is called to follow in Christ's footsteps, but never on one's own. Faith's love goes out from and always returns to the fullness of the divine life. Murray Rae sums up Kierkegaard's perspective in this way: "Venturing the decisive act of imitation becomes the means by which the disciple 'flees to grace.'"[192]

Of course, *Practice in Christianity* is not the only place where Kierkegaard discusses Christ as *Forbillede*. It is arguably the defining motif of his later authorship, surfacing in works such as *Upbuilding Discourses in Various Spirits* (1847), *Christian Discourses* (1848), and *For Self-Examination* (1851), not to mention the posthumously published *Judge for Yourself!* (1876). Whether this "turn" represents a valuable outgrowth of, or a shameful deviation from, Kierkegaard's earlier thinking has been widely debated.[193] The crucial point in this context is that Kierkegaard situates Christ's *Billede*—or *icons* of Christ—at the center of his later writings. To read these works is to enter

190. SKS 12, 196 / PC, 197–98.
191. More precisely, faith's humility, suffering, and love come together in the imitation of Christ. Thus one might say that the theme of *imitatio Christi* encapsulates each aspect of faith. Doubtless that is why Kierkegaard devoted so much attention to it.
192. Murray Rae, *Kierkegaard and Theology* (London: T & T Clark, 2010), 82. Also see SKS 23, 399, NB20:15 / JP 2, 1785.
193. Again, for a fuller discussion of this issue, see my book *Kierkegaard, Pietism and Holiness* (Farnham: Ashgate, 2011).

into an imaginative space, where Christ, exemplifying faith's love, is presented as a picture for contemplation.

Yet again, as with any good iconographer, Kierkegaard is clear that the *Tegn* of Christ is intended neither for indifferent assessment nor for mere admiration. Such are the ways of the idol, in which the image is reduced to an immanent value or end. For that reason, Kierkegaard avers that the contemplation of Christ's image, properly understood, must be open to the possibility of faith and, with it, union with Love itself—the Love that shines on the just and the unjust, on friend and foe, on all creation.[194] Christ himself embodies this love, and so the believer follows him in loving God and neighbor. Love is not only an aspect of faith, but its fruition.[195]

In this way, Kierkegaard gestures toward another classic theme in Christian spirituality, namely, the relation between the life of contemplation [*vita contemplativa*] and that of action [*vita activa*]. As has been seen, Kierkegaard underlines the import of the former, but always with an eye toward realizing the latter. Like a modern-day Francis of Assisi,[196] Kierkegaard refuses to grant priority to the *vita contemplativa* over the *vita activa*. In fact, he implicitly rejects the view, typical in the patristic era, that the "contemplative life [is] higher and more desirable" than its active counterpart, even if the latter is "more pressing due to the obligations of Christian love."[197] Kierkegaard's recommendation, rather, would seem to resemble the

---

194. See Matt. 5:45.

195. In a sense, then, I agree with Pattison's suggestion that "Kierkegaard himself, as a religious thinker, is more adequately understood as an expositor of the love of God than as a defender of the faith" (George Pattison, *The Philosophy of Kierkegaard* [Chesham: Acumen, 2005], 164), since the Anti-Climacan conception of faith as a more-than-propositional grounding in the divine life does, indeed, culminate in love. And yet, unlike Pattison, I would not want to go so far as to say that, for Kierkegaard, "the tap-root of religious existence is not to be found in 'faith' or 'belief' at all" (Ibid.). As I have tried to show, Kierkegaard is deeply suspicious of a merely propositional account of faith, while also insisting that faith, as a state of being-with-God, is necessary for the flowering of love.

196. See, for example, Kenneth Baxter Wolf, *The Poverty of Riches: St. Francis of Assisi Reconsidered* (Oxford: Oxford University Press, 2003).

ideal of "active while in contemplation" [*in contemplatione activus*].[198] To be sure, his own emphasis on "contemporaneity," which might be defined as "a relationship with Christ made present in faith,"[199] suggests a transition from contemplating the "sign of contradiction" to encountering Christ in the actuality of everyday life. As Anti-Climacus opens *Practice in Christianity*:

> [C]ontemporaneity is the condition of faith, and, more sharply defined, it is faith. Lord Jesus Christ, would that we, too, might become contemporary with you in this way, might see you in your true form and in the surroundings of actuality as you walked here on earth. . . . Would that we might see you as you are and were and will be until your second coming in glory, as the sign of offense and the object of faith, the lowly man, yet the Savior and Redeemer of the human race, who out of love came to earth to seek the lost. . . .[200]

Nevertheless, this sort of spirituality may seem daunting to many, fanciful to others. Held up as an icon of faith's love, Christ's example might still seem too lofty or too aloof for imitation. How is an ordinary person—indeed, a sinner—supposed to follow after the *Forbillede* of Jesus? Kierkegaard addresses this question with his discourses on the woman who was a sinner, who stands as another icon of faith's love.

By Way of Conclusion: The Woman Who Was a Sinner

Over the last several years of his life, Kierkegaard wrestled a great deal with the problem of *imitatio Christi*. To reduplicate the love

197. Bernard McGinn, "Contemplation and Action," in *The Essential Writings of Christian Mysticism*, ed. Bernard McGinn (New York: Modern Library, 2006), 520.
198. Ibid.
199. This definition is largely taken from Watkin, *Kierkegaard's Philosophy*, 56, though, in order to bring out Kierkegaard's understanding of contemporaneity, I have added the words "made present."
200. SKS 12, 17 / PC, 9–10.

of Christ, he reasoned, represents the apex of Christian existence. And yet, few actually achieve this ideal—a problem only exacerbated by Christendom, which, in tempering the demands of Christianity, would reduce the faith to an arm of the nation-state. It was for that reason, of course, that Kierkegaard lashed out at Denmark's state church. As he argued, when faith terminates in Danish citizenship, rather than in Christian love, its *raison d'être* is nullified.

At the same time, however, Kierkegaard was sensitive to the claim that he sought to make Christianity tantamount to the suffering and martyrdom of Christ—a charge leveled against him by allies of the state church as well as by later critics. Marie Mikulová Thulstrup has summed up this complaint pithily, contending that, for Kierkegaard, "[Christ as] Pattern points the way to martyrdom; it is the Christian's destiny."[201] Nevertheless, Kierkegaard rejects this view in both his published and private writings. In the latter, he repeatedly stresses that by no means is he *requiring* a particular expression of Christian love, since, after all, "[a] man is capable of nothing at all—it is grace alone."[202] Instead, he is simply asking persons to open themselves up to the activity of divine grace, which is the *sine qua non* of the imitation of Christ.[203] Likewise, in "Does a Human Being Have the Right to Let Himself Be Put to Death for the Truth?," H. H. concludes that the only martyrdom permissible in Christendom is that of one who refuses to seek martyrdom.[204] This assertion has the appearance of a joke, but H. H. is calling to mind the example of Christ himself, who did not pursue the cross but, with humble simplicity, merely submitted to divine Providence.[205]

---

201. Marie Mikulová Thulstrup, "Kierkegaard's Dialectic of Imitation," in *A Kierkegaard Critique: An International Selection of Essays Interpreting Kierkegaard*, ed. Howard A. Johnson and Niels Thulstrup (New York: Harper, 1962), 277.
202. SKS 24, NB 22:159 / JP 2, 1482.
203. SKS 25, NB 27:8 / JP 2, 1489.
204. SKS 11, 89 / WA, 85.

In the end, then, Kierkegaard's invocation of *imitatio Christi* essentially concerns Christ's passivity—that is to say, his desire to *rest* in the will of God. This example is all the more pertinent in light of human sin, which ensures that holiness can never be attained but only received. In fact, it is precisely when one comes to realize this point that one is poised to resemble Christ. As Kierkegaard writes,

> If I were to define Christian perfection, I should not say that it is a perfection of striving but specifically that it is the deep recognition of the imperfection of one's striving, and precisely because of this a deeper and deeper consciousness of the need for grace, not grace for this or that, but the infinite need infinitely for grace.[206]

In this comment, Kierkegaard alludes to a number of themes discussed in this work—the possibility of authentic selfhood, the inherent tension within the self, the progressive unfolding of spiritual truth, and, finally, the need to rest in God. In turn, he sets the stage for what could be his most significant "icon of faith," the woman who was a sinner.

Kierkegaard mentions "the sinner woman" [*Synderinden*] in three discourses—an early piece entitled "Love Will Hide a Multitude of Sins" (1843), along with more substantive treatments in "The Woman Who Was a Sinner" (1849) and "An Upbuilding Discourse" (1850). All draw from Luke 7:36-50, which, famously, tells of Jesus' encounter with a sinful woman at the home of a Pharisee. This gospel passage is also showcased in *Two Discourses at the Communion of Fridays* (1851).[207] Although Kierkegaard does not name the woman

---

205. See, e.g., Luke 22:42: "Father, if you are willing, remove this cup from me; yet, not my will but yours be done."
206. NB 22:159 / JP 2, 1482.
207. It is worth adding that the second of these two discourses is also known as "Love Will Hide a Multitude of Sins," further connecting *Two Discourses at the Communion of Fridays* to the sinner woman.

who was a sinner in this work, one might argue that her presence is implicit—the form intimated by the content.

Already, then, it is clear that Kierkegaard had a penchant for this biblical figure. Yet, his fondness was not only personal; it indicates notable conceptual links as well. That is to say, with the exception of the 1843 discourse, Kierkegaard clustered his icons of the sinner woman around the Anti-Climacan writings. He makes this connection explicit in an 1849 journal entry,[208] and it is further implied by Kierkegaard's insistence that *Two Discourses at the Communion of Fridays*, though issued in 1851, be attributed to 1849—the year of *The Sickness unto Death*'s publication.[209] Similarly, "An Upbuilding Discourse" dates from 1850 and, so, corresponds to the release of *Practice in Christianity*. These convergences suggest that the theoretical work accomplished by Anti-Climacus is, in some way, fleshed out in Kierkegaard's icons of *Synderinden*.

That is not to dismiss, however, the 1843 version of "Love Will Hide a Multitude of Sins." In this early discourse, as well as in its predecessor of the same name, much of Kierkegaard's thinking on the sinner woman is anticipated. He opens the first discourse with a touching paean to love:

> What is it that is older than everything? It is love [*Kjerlighed*]. What is it that outlives everything? It is love. What is it that cannot be taken but itself takes all? It is love. What is it that cannot be given but itself gives all? It is love. . . . What is it that endures when everything is changed? It is love. What is it that remains when the imperfect is abolished? It is love. What is it that witnesses when prophecy is silent? It is love.[210]

208. SKS 22, NB 13:57 / JP 6, 6515. This entry was also noted earlier, albeit with regard to the tax collector.
209. SKS 12, 278 / WA, 162. Also see *Pap.* X 5 B 132 / WA, 270.
210. SKS 5, 65–66 / EUD, 55.

Yet, Kierkegaard goes on, this understanding of love is not universal. It is not extolled in paganism, nor is it fully developed in the Hebrew Scriptures.[211] Rather, it enters the world with Jesus Christ, who incarnates and inculcates a radical form of love—"that which blesses and blesses when it is cursed, that which loves its neighbor but whose enemy is also its neighbor, that which leaves revenge to the Lord because it takes comfort in the thought that he is even more merciful."[212] It is *this* love that "covers a multitude of sins" (1 Pet. 4:8).

But how? Intriguingly, Kierkegaard notes that *Kjerlighed* is best understood in relation to the faculty of vision. The one who loves sees love in the world, just as the one who hates sees hatred. For seeing is not just a physical capacity, but a spiritual one as well: "A person's inner being . . . determines what he discovers and what he hides."[213] But this effect cannot be reduced to an interior, private experience. When love sees love in the sinner, "this eye sees not the impure but the pure, which it loves and loves forth by loving it."[214] In this way, love "translates evil into good . . ."[215]

Kierkegaard admits that this may seem like "beautiful yet futile speech."[216] After all, the world is far from perfect, and those who love all too often suffer at the hands of those who don't. And yet, "[p]erhaps the understanding merely lacked the courage to believe [*at troe*]"[217] in love. If everyone believed in love, perhaps the world would be different, for "love gives unbounded courage."[218] In closing, Kierkegaard cites the example of Christ, whose love, even in the

---

211. SKS 5, 66 / EUD, 55–56. Of course, whether or not Kierkegaard is right on this point is another question.
212. SKS 5, 67 / EUD, 57.
213. SKS 5, 70 / EUD, 60.
214. SKS 5, 71 / EUD, 61.
215. SKS 5, 71 / EUD, 61.
216. SKS 5, 74 / EUD, 65.
217. SKS 5, 75 / EUD, 65.
218. SKS 5, 75 / EUD, 65.

midst of hostility, finds love in the other and, in turn, secures forgiveness.[219]

The first discourse, then, establishes Christ as the one whose love hides the sins of others; however, Kierkegaard takes a somewhat different approach in its successor. Now he looks at the matter from the perspective of the sinner. Isn't it the case, he asks, that love at times *discovers* sinfulness, as when a person, formerly carefree, falls in love and suddenly realizes how inadequate he really is?[220] Or might not a person, otherwise confident in her moral decency, cower when confronted with God's eternal love, which diminishes her accomplishments and magnifies her faults? Indeed, this is as it should be, for "[l]ove is no fantasy."[221] Like childbirth, it does not give without pain: "Love takes everything. It takes a person's perfection . . . but it also takes his imperfection, his sin, his distress. It takes away his strength, but also his suffering . . ."[222] For that reason, the one who encounters love must detach from both perfection and imperfection, from self-righteousness as well as from self-condemnation. Only then does *love* reign; only then does the person *rest* in love.

This sort of love is daunting, particularly for the sinner. But the more one believes in love, the more one "sees only love and the blessedness of paradise."[223] With this in mind, Kierkegaard turns his attention to the woman who was a sinner. To approach Jesus at all, he surmises, must have been hard for her, since the "accusations of her own heart"[224] told her that she was unworthy of his friendship. That she did so amid the Pharisees, who disdained her, only added to her apprehension. "But she went on, and in beating the enemy she

219. SKS 5, 77 / EUD, 68.
220. SKS 5, 81–82 / EUD, 73.
221. SKS 5, 82 / EUD, 73, my translation.
222. SKS 5, 82 / EUD, 74.
223. SKS 5, 84 / EUD, 75.
224. SKS 5, 84 / EUD 75.

beat herself to calmness [*Ro*], and when she had found rest [*Hvile*] at Jesus' feet, she forgot herself in her work of love."[225] Thus the sinner woman's faith in and longing for love (Christ) overcame her sins as well as those of others. "She was forgiven her many sins, because she loved much."[226] If the goal of the spiritual life is to rest in God, the woman who was a sinner shows that it produces a salutary effect—namely, the "peacefulness [*Hvile*] of love."[227]

This story, as Kierkegaard concludes, shocks precisely to the extent that it contradicts social convention. Society establishes certain laws and holds persons accountable to those standards. But love has only one requirement, and that is to love. As Kierkegaard puts it, "[I]f we continue in love, who is it, then, who accuses?"[228] Once one has yielded to the sway of love, there is nothing left to fear. Thus Kierkegaard returns to the woman who was a sinner:

> The judgment of the world was legible on the faces of the Pharisees; it could not be deceived; her sorrow and her tears concealed nothing but disclosed everything, and there was nothing to discover but a multitude of sins. She was not seeking the world's judgment, however, "but she stood behind Jesus at his feet and wept." Then *love* discovered what the world concealed—the love in her; and since it had not been victorious in

---

225. SKS 5, 84 / EUD, 75.

226. SKS 5, 84 / EUD, 76.

227. SKS 5, 84 / EUD, 76.

228. SKS 5, 85 / EUD, 77. This line of reasoning echoes Augustine of Hippo's famous statement, "Love, and do what you want." See Saint Augustine, *Homilies on the First Epistle of John*, trans. Boniface Ramsey (Hyde Park, NY: New City Press, 2008), 110. This similarity should not be surprising. As mentioned in Chapter Two, Lee C. Barrett has recently explored the connections between Augustine and Kierkegaard, noting that both thinkers stress the final unity of "[d]ivine agape and human eros" (Barrett, *The Intersections of Augustine and Kierkegaard*, 25). For that reason, Barrett later notes, the two thinkers essentially identify sanctification with love, since holiness is nothing other than "the actualization of the loving mutuality that will be our ultimate fulfillment" (Ibid., 392). This point sheds light on this text's portrayal of Kierkegaardian faith. As has been emphasized, Kierkegaard is not content to view faith in merely forensic terms but, rather, sees it as having a kind of "form," comprised of humility, suffering, and love. That, indeed, is why it lends itself so readily to iconic rendering. With this in mind, it is worth adding that, like me, Barrett concludes that Kierkegaard and Balthasar actually shared "a similar vision" (Ibid., 25), the latter's protestations notwithstanding.

her, the Savior's love came to her assistance . . . and he made the love in her even more powerful to hide a multitude of sins. . . .[229]

With this statement, Kierkegaard effectively sums up the pair of discourses. Christ's love is the original and immutable love, which discovers love in everyone. That this love has such primacy will offend many. Yet, for those who respond to it, it will awaken the love already in them and draw them into a deeper participation in Love itself—a response imaged by the sinner woman.

Indeed, returning to *Synderinden* several years later, Kierkegaard makes her iconic status certain. "The Woman Who Was a Sinner" begins by recapitulating a number of crucial themes, not only from the 1843 versions of "Love Will Hide a Multitude of Sins," but from other upbuilding discourses too. For example, the necessity of confession, so important in *Upbuilding Discourses in Various Spirits*, is reprised.[230] Even more significantly, Kierkegaard touches on the self's need to become "nothing" before God, as exemplified by the woman's willingness to express her faith in and love for Christ in a hostile environment—a topic that goes back to "To Need God is a Human Being's Highest Perfection,"[231] not to mention its mystical forerunners. Moreover, the import of this nothingness comes into sharper focus, since, as Kierkegaard underlines, Christianity requires a particular form of self-abasement, namely, a love orientated wholly toward the other, like the "one who in mortal danger forgets himself and lets the other have the only life-saving plank . . ."[232] Of course, this is the love embodied by Christ, but, in her profound love for the Savior, it comes to radiate in the sinner woman as well. She has become an icon of faith:

229. SKS 5, 86 / EUD, 77.
230. SKS 11, 275 / WA, 139.
231. SKS 11, 276 / WA, 140.
232. SKS 11, 277 / WA, 141.

> She says nothing and therefore is not what she says, but she is what she does not say, or what she does not say is what she is. She *is* the symbol, like a picture [*Billede*]. She has forgotten speech and language and the restlessness [*Uro*], has forgotten what is even greater restlessness, this self, has forgotten herself—she, the lost woman, who is now lost in her Savior, who, lost in him, rests [*hviler*] at his feet—like a picture.[233]

So luminous is this iconic quality that, as Kierkegaard imagines it, Christ himself recognized it in her: "It is almost as if the Savior himself momentarily looked at her and the situation that way, as if she were not an actual person but a picture."[234] Kierkegaard finds evidence of this gesture in the biblical text itself, noting that, as Luke records it, Jesus "does not speak *to* her . . . but *about* her . . . almost as if he changed her into a picture . . ."[235]

To call the sinner woman a *Billede* is to accentuate the timelessness of her example. The image of her humbled before Christ, bathing his feet with her tears, "is more inciting than all rhetorical incitements."[236] The overwhelming love of God, the self's thirst for spiritual wholeness, the antagonism of a world captive to its own idolatry—all of these are present in the "eternal picture"[237] of the woman who was a sinner, "she who therefore also found rest [*Hvile*] for her soul in loving much . . ."[238] In her, finally, faith and love are indistinguishable; they both issue in the peace of resting in God.

Published roughly a year later, "An Upbuilding Discourse" furthers the status of the sinner woman. Not only is she a noteworthy figure, but now she perdures as a "teacher" and "prototype of piety."[239] Kierkegaard admits that, given her gender, such a claim may seem

233. SKS 11, 277 / WA, 141.
234. SKS 11, 277 / WA, 141.
235. SKS 11, 277 / WA, 141.
236. SKS 11, 280 / WA, 144.
237. SKS 11, 279 / WA, 143.
238. SKS 11, 280 / WA, 144.
239. SKS 12, 263 / WA, 149.

surprising, but he adds that "piety or godliness is fundamentally womanliness."[240] This is a curious assertion at best, and Kierkegaard's views on women have, in approbation and in criticism, garnered a degree of attention in the secondary literature.[241] Here, to be sure, his essentialist language begs the question and would rightly fail to pass muster in contemporary discourse. Nevertheless, it must be noted that Kierkegaard is directing his opinion *against* the patriarchal norms obtaining in nineteenth-century society. In other words, where his peers would tend to equate godliness with masculinity—citing, as examples, the early church fathers and the restrictions placed on ecclesial ordination—Kierkegaard says just the opposite. To be a Christian is not about attaining an institutional position or assuming control over others; it has to do with being *receptive* to God—a quality he associates with femininity,[242] not least because, in his day, women had to learn to accept the ebb and flow of civic life. This was surely a disadvantage in social matters, yet, Kierkegaard insists, it disposes women to better understand the nature of Christian spirituality, which, for women *and* for men, is realized only in an attitude of quiet self-effacement before God. Anti-Climacus calls this state "faith," and, in "An Upbuilding Discourse," Kierkegaard echoes this point:

> From a woman, therefore, you also learn the humble faith in relation to the extraordinary, the humble faith that does not incredulously, doubtingly ask, "Why? What for? How is this possible?"—but as Mary humbly believes and says, "Behold, I am the handmaid of the Lord." She

240. SKS 12, 263 / WA, 149.
241. See, for example, *Feminist Interpretations of Søren Kierkegaard*, ed. Céline Léon and Sylvia Walsh (University Park: Pennsylvania State University Press, 1997) and Céline Léon, *The Neither/Nor of the Second Sex: Kierkegaard on Women, Sexual Difference, and Sexual Relations* (Macon, GA: Mercer University Press, 2008).
242. In *The Sickness unto Death*, however, Anti-Climacus adds that there is a form of despair characteristic of the feminine, in effect, to fail to self-actualize, to submit to despair rather than to God. See, for example, SKS 11, 165 / SUD, 49–50. This form of despair is the mirror image of the sinner woman—a point that hints at a further connection between *The Sickness unto Death* and his late writings on *Synderinden*.

says this, but note that to say this is actually to be silent. From a woman you learn the proper hearing of the Word. . . .[243]

If, for Kierkegaard, Christ remains the ultimate "icon of faith," here he reiterates that Christ's *Forbillede* is met only by following figures such as Mary and the sinner woman. Just where a "masculine" mindset might presume to mimic Christ's example, to come forward as a religious hero over against a fallen world, these "feminine" prototypes remind one that godliness is strictly a matter of being open to God.[244] One cannot *will* holiness; it can only be let in.

These points underlie the remainder of "An Upbuilding Discourse," which goes on to clarify how persons can learn from the sinner woman. First, Kierkegaard notes that she represents the proper way to sorrow over one's sins. Neither assuming that God's mercy is weaker than her failures, nor defiantly claiming sin as her life's principle, she simply seeks the forgiveness found in Christ. In this pursuit, she does not evince the reckless audacity of despair but the quiet concentration of faith: "[S]he . . . is not in despair, she is a believer. And so she enters, indifferent to everything else. Yet this . . . does not create any sensation, any uproar, because she is a believer and therefore so quiet, modest, and humble . . ."[245]

Part of this single-mindedness, Kierkegaard continues, is the sinner woman's recognition that "*she herself is able to do nothing at all.*"[246] She is no longer occupied with the myriad of distractions that constitute

---

243. SKS 12, 263 / WA, 149.
244. Kierkegaard's use of the term, "godliness" [*Gudelighed*] subtly intensifies this claim. More than a mere synonym for "piety" [*Fromhed*], it is a word that, in Danish, literally means "God-likeness." Hence, in designating the woman who was a sinner as a prototype of *Gudelighed*, Kierkegaard is underlining that one is most like God when one gives oneself over to him in faith's humility, suffering, and love. Put in traditional theological language, Kierkegaard insists that grace is needed to elevate human nature to divinity, though persons must nevertheless cooperate with its activity.
245. SKS 12, 268 / WA, 154.
246. SKS 12, 268 / WA, 155.

despair, from concerns over her standing in the eyes of others to fantastical dreams about escaping her present situation. She understands that what she really wants is the calm [Ro] that can only come from being grounded in God. Yet, for just that reason, it is a calm that she cannot procure herself: she cannot earn it (for it is always on offer), nor can she produce (for it is of God). Thus she empties herself of all pretensions and becomes nothing before God:

> She enters. She fully understands that she herself is able to do nothing. She does not for that reason abandon herself to expressions of passionate self-accusation, as if that would bring her closer to salvation or make her more pleasing to God. She does not exaggerate—indeed, no one can charge her with that. No, she does nothing at all, she is silent—she weeps.[247]

But even her tears, Kierkegaard points out, are a sign of her self-dispossession, for crying is not fabricated but *elicited*. She has, in short, succumbed to the divine. With this in mind, Kierkegaard returns to the core of his theological anthropology, as outlined in Chapter Two. God is the eternal and immutable source of all creaturely activity, who remains ever open to and operative for the return of the human being: "[B]*efore* God, a person is capable of nothing at all. How would it even be possible, since, after all, even in connection with the slightest thing of which a person is capable, humanly speaking, he is capable of nothing except *through* God!"[248] To see the image of the woman who was a sinner is to see a picture of this insight.

And yet, as an icon of faith, it retains a twofold distance. That Jesus is the Son of God cannot be pictured. That his love redeems the sinner woman, reuniting her with God, remains beyond representation. The one contemplating this icon, then, must do so with care. It does not provide the easy comfort of the idol, which

247. SKS 12, 269 / WA, 156.
248. SKS 12, 271 / WA, 158.

would tender the happy ending of a Hollywood film, but leaves one with the uneasy realization that all of Christ's followers—even the woman who was a sinner[249]—failed to see him properly at some point. "[A]s the prototype, no human being can hold out with [Christ] entirely; they all fall away, even the apostles."[250] Hence, as Kierkegaard himself did, one must keep returning to the picture, opening oneself up to its excessive significance, waiting for its disclosure of joy amid pain.

In other words, there is "comfort" in the image of the sinner woman, but "[it] is only for faith."[251] This is the last line of "An Upbuilding Discourse,"[252] and it serves as a fitting conclusion to this study as well. For Kierkegaard, faith is never a blind wish, and it is always more than a creedal assent. It is, as his various icons show, the focal point of the spiritual life—a disposition that views the world with wide-eyed honesty, humble about one's limitations, willing to suffer the vicissitudes of life, and continually believing in and looking for the love that undergirds and animates all creation. To be sure, one may fall away from faith: this is despair. Yet, in the manner of the sinner woman and others, a return to faith and its rest ever beckons. It beckons not only via the natural world and its iconic beauty, but also via the Bible and its motley cast of characters, who, for centuries, have been pictured for the sake of Christian upbuilding. More than just a "thinker," Kierkegaard belongs to this tradition as well, his icons of faith summing up his most enduring spiritual insights, even as they draw one toward "the peace of God, which surpasses all understanding" (Phil. 4:7).

249. SKS 12, 272 / WA, 159.
250. SKS 12, 272 / WA, 159.
251. SKS 12, 273 / WA, 160.
252. Kierkegaard seems to have wanted to end with a play on words, juxtaposing the Danish terms for "comfort" [*Trøst*] and "faith" [*Troen*]—a similarity whose significance would not have been lost on him, who, as has been seen, spilled more than a little ink on how faith leads to rest and, so, to comfort.

Works Cited

Works by Søren Kierkegaard

In Danish

Søren Kierkegaards Papirer. Edited by P. A. Heiberg, V. Kuhr, and E. Torsting. 11 vols. iii. Copenhagen: Gyldendalske Boghandel, 1909–48.

Søren Kierkegaards Skrifter. Edited by Niels Jørgen Cappelørn, Joakim Garff, Johnny Kondrup, Karsten Kynde, Tonny Aagaard Olesen, and Steen Tullberg. Copenhagen: Gads Forlag, 1997–2013.

In English

Søren Kierkegaard's Journals and Papers. Edited and translated by Howard Hong and Edna Hong. 7 vols. Bloomington: Indiana University Press, 1967–78.

Kierkegaard's Writings. Edited and translated by Howard Hong and Edna Hong. 26 vols. Princeton, NJ: Princeton University Press, 1978–2002.

Kierkegaard's Journals and Notebooks. Edited by Niels Jørgen Cappelørn, Alastair Hannay, David Kangas, Bruce H. Kirmmse, George Pattison, Vanessa Rumble, and K. Brian Söderquist. 11 vols. Princeton, NJ: Princeton University Press, 2007–.

Other Sources

Anderson, Thomas C. "Is the Religion of *Eighteen Upbuilding Discourses* Religiousness A?" In *International Kierkegaard Commentary: Eighteen Upbuilding Discourses*, edited by Robert L. Perkins, 51-75. Macon, GA: Mercer University Press, 2003.

Arndt, Johann. *True Christianity.* Translated by Peter C. Erb. New York: Paulist, 1979.

Auden, W. H. "Presenting Kierkegaard." In *The Living Thoughts of Kierkegaard*, edited by W. H. Auden, 3-22. Bloomington: Indiana University Press, 1952.

Baagø, Kaj. *Vækkelse og Kirkeliv i København og Omegn.* Copenhagen: Gads Forlag, 1960.

Ballan, Joseph. "Hans Urs von Balthasar: Persuasive Forms or Offensive Signs? Kierkegaard and the Problems of Theological Aesthetics." In *Kierkegaard's Influence on Theology: Tome III: Catholic and Jewish Theology*, edited by Jon Stewart, 3-24. Farnham: Ashgate Publishing, 2012.

Balthasar, Hans Urs von. *The Glory of the Lord: A Theological Aesthetics.* Volume 1. Translated by Erasmo Leiva-Merikakis. San Francisco: Ignatius Press, 1982.

Barnett, Christopher B. *Kierkegaard, Pietism and Holiness.* Farnham: Ashgate, 2011.

———. "The Mystical Influence on Kierkegaard's Theological Anthropology." *Acta Kierkegaardiana* 6 (2013): 105–22.

———. "Erich Przywara, S.J.: Catholicism's Great Expositor of the 'Mystery' of Kierkegaard." In *Kierkegaard's Influence on Theology: Tome III: Catholic and Jewish Theology*, edited by Jon Stewart, 131-51. Farnham: Ashgate Publishing, 2012.

———. "Catholicism." In *Kierkegaard's Concepts: Absolute to Church*, edited by Steven M. Emmanuel, William McDonald and Jon Stewart, 161-66. Farnham: Ashgate Publishing, 2013.

Barrett, Lee C. *Eros and Self-Emptying: The Intersections of Augustine and Kierkegaard*. Grand Rapids, MI: Eerdmans, 2013.

Bernard of Clairvaux. "On Loving God." In *Bernard of Clairvaux: Selected Works*, translated by G.R. Evans, 173–205. New York: Paulist, 1987.

Bloom, Harold. *Genius: A Mosaic of One Hundred Exemplary Creative Minds*. New York: Warner Books, 2002.

Boring, M. Eugene. "The Gospel of Matthew: An Introduction, Commentary, and Reflections." In *The New Interpreter's Bible: A Commentary in Twelve Volumes*, vol. 8, 87–505. Nashville: Abingdon, 1995.

Clapper, Gregory S. "Relations Between Spirituality and Theology: Kierkegaard's Model." *Studies in Formative Spirituality* 9 [1988]: 161-67.

Come, Arnold B. *Kierkegaard as Humanist: Discovering My Self.* Montreal: McGill-Queen's University Press, 1995.

Cruysberghs, Paul. "Transparency to Oneself and to God." In *At være sig selv nærværende: Festskrift til Niels Jørgen Cappelørn*, edited by Joakim Garff,

Ettore Rocca, and Pia Søltoft, 127–41. Copenhagen: Kristeligt Dagblads Forlag, 2010.

Dewey, Bradley R. *The New Obedience: Kierkegaard on Imitating Christ.* Washington, DC: Corpus Books, 1968.

Dostoevsky, Fyodor. *The Brothers Karamazov.* Translated by Richard Pevear and Larissa Volokhonsky. New York: Knopf, 1992.

Eckhart, Meister. "On the Noble Man." In *Meister Eckhart: Selected Writings,* translated by Oliver Davies, 97–108. New York: Penguin Books, 1994.

Edwards, Jonathan. "Jonathan Edwards on the Beauty of Creation." In *The Christian Theology Reader,* edited by Alister E. McGrath, 122–23. Oxford: Blackwell Publishing, 2007.

Evans, C. Stephens. *Kierkegaard: An Introduction.* Cambridge: Cambridge University Press, 2009.

———. *Søren Kierkegaard's Christian Psychology: Insight for Counseling and Pastoral Care.* Vancouver: Regent College Publishing, 1990.

Fabro, Cornelio. "Influssi Cattolici Sulla Spiritualità Kierkegaardiana." *Humanitas* 17 (1962): 501-07.

Ferreira, M. Jamie. *Love's Grateful Striving: A Commentary on Kierkegaard's Works of Love.* Oxford: Oxford University Press, 2001.

Forest, Jim. *Praying with Icons.* Maryknoll, NY: Orbis Books, 2008.

Gallagher, Michael Paul. "Faith." In *The New Westminster Dictionary of Christian Spirituality,* edited by Philip Sheldrake, 297–98. Louisville: Westminster John Knox, 2005.

Garff, Joakim. *Søren Kierkegaard: A Biography*. Translated by Bruce H. Kirmmse. Princeton, NJ: Princeton University Press, 2005.

Green, Ronald M. "'Developing' in *Fear and Trembling*." In *The Cambridge Companion to Kierkegaard*, edited by Alastair Hannay and Gordon D. Marino, 257–81. Cambridge: Cambridge University Press, 1998.

Gschwandtner, Christina M. *Reading Jean-Luc Marion: Exceeding Metaphysics*. Bloomington: Indiana University Press, 2007.

Hampson, Daphne. *Christian Contradictions: The Structures of Lutheran and Catholic Thought*. Cambridge: Cambridge University Press, 2001.

Hannay, Alastair. *Kierkegaard: A Biography*. Cambridge: Cambridge University Press, 2001.

Heidegger, Martin. *Identity and Difference*. Translated by Joan Stambaugh. New York: Harper & Row, 1969.

Hong, Howard and Edna. "Historical Introduction." In *Eighteen Upbuilding Discourses*, edited by Howard V. Hong and Edna H. Hong, ix-xxii. Princeton, NJ: Princeton University Press, 1990.

———. "Historical Introduction." In *Three Discourses on Imagined Occasions*, edited and translated by Howard V. Hong and Edna H. Hong, vii–xiii. Princeton, NJ: Princeton University Press, 1993.

———. "Historical Introduction." In *Without Authority*, edited by Howard V. Hong and Edna H. Hong, ix–xix. Princeton, NJ: Princeton University Press, 1997.

Hopkins, Gerard Manley. "God's Grandeur." In *God's Grandeur and Other Poems*, 15. Mineola, NY: Dover, 1995.

Howland, Garth A. "John Valentine Haidt: A Little Known Eighteenth Century Painter." *Pennsylvania History* 8, no. 4 (1941): 303–13.

Kingo, Anders. *Den Opbyggelige Tale: En systematisk-teologisk studie over Søren Kierkegaards opbyggelige forfatterskab.* Copenhagen: Gad, 1987.

Kodalle, Klaus-M. "The Utilitarian Self and the 'Useless' Passion of Faith." In *The Cambridge Companion to Kierkegaard,* edited by Alastair Hannay and Gordon D. Marino, 397-410. Cambridge: Cambridge University Press, 1998.

Laird, Martin. *Into the Silent Land: A Guide to the Christian Practice of Contemplation.* Oxford: Oxford University Press, 2006.

Law, David R. *Kierkegaard's Kenotic Christology.* Oxford: Oxford University Press, 2013.

Léon, Céline, and Sylvia Walsh, eds. *Feminist Interpretations of Søren Kierkegaard.* University Park: Pennsylvania State University Press, 1997.

Léon, Céline. *The Neither/Nor of the Second Sex: Kierkegaard on Women, Sexual Difference, and Sexual Relations.* Macon, GA: Mercer University Press, 2008.

Libera, Alain de. *Albert le Grand et la philosophie.* Paris: Vrin, 1990.

Limouris, Gennadios. "The Microcosm and Macrocosm of the Icon: Theology, Spirituality and Worship in Colour." In *Icons, Windows on Eternity: Theology and Spirituality in Colour,* 93–123. Geneva: WCC Publications, 1990.

Lindberg, Carter. Introduction to *The Pietist Theologians,* edited by Carter Lindberg, 1–20. Oxford: Wiley-Blackwell, 2005.

Marion, Jean-Luc. *God without Being*. Translated by Thomas A. Carlson. Chicago: University of Chicago Press, 1991.

McGinn, Bernard. *The Essential Writings of Christian Mysticism*. New York: Modern Library, 2006.

McGrath, Alister E. *Christian Spirituality: An Introduction*. Oxford: Blackwell, 1999.

Mulder, Jr., Jack. *Kierkegaard and the Catholic Tradition: Conflict and Dialogue*. Bloomington, IN: Indiana University Press, 2010.

Müller, Paul. "Begrebet 'det Opbyggelige' hos Søren Kierkegaard." *Fønix* 7 (1983): 1-16.

Pattison, George. *Kierkegaard: The Aesthetic and the Religious: From the Magic Theatre to the Crucifixion of the Image*. New York: St. Martin's, 1992.

———. *Kierkegaard and the Crisis of Faith: An Introduction to His Thought*. London: SPCK, 1997.

———. "Art in an Age of Reflection." In *The Cambridge Companion to Kierkegaard*, edited by Alastair Hannay and Gordon D. Marino, 76–100. Cambridge: Cambridge University Press, 1998.

———. *Kierkegaard's Upbuilding Discourses: Philosophy, Literature and Theology*. London: Routledge, 2002.

———. *The Philosophy of Kierkegaard*. Chesham: Acumen, 2005.

———. Foreword to *Kierkegaard: Spiritual Writings*, translated by George Pattison, xi–xxvii. New York: Harper Perennial, 2010.

Podmore, Simon D. *Kierkegaard and the Self Before God*. Bloomington: Indiana University Press, 2011.

————. *Struggling with God: Kierkegaard and the Temptation of Spiritual Trial.* Cambridge: James Clarke & Co., 2013.

Polk, Timothy Houston. *The Biblical Kierkegaard: Reading by the Rule of Faith.* Macon, GA: Mercer University Press, 1997.

Przywara, Erich. *Das Geheimnis Kierkegaards.* Munich and Berlin: Verlag von R. Oldenbourg, 1929.

Rae, Murray. *Kierkegaard's Vision of the Incarnation: By Faith Transformed.* Oxford: Clarendon, 1997.

————. *Kierkegaard and Theology.* London: T & T Clark, 2010.

Rose, Timothy. *Kierkegaard's Christocentric Theology.* Aldershot: Ashgate, 2001.

Šajda, Peter. "Kierkegaard's Encounter with Rhineland-Flemish Mystics: A Case Study." In *Kierkegaard Studies Yearbook 2009: Kierkegaard's Concept of Irony*, edited by Niels Jørgen Cappelørn, Hermann Deuser, and K. Brian Söderquist, 559-84. Berlin: de Gruyter, 2009.

Saint Augustine. *Confessions.* Translated by R. S. Pine-Coffin. London: Penguin Books, 1961.

————. *Homilies on the First Epistle of John.* Translated by Boniface Ramsey. Hyde Park, NY: New City Press, 2008.

Sampley, J. Paul. "The First Letter to the Corinthians." In *The New Interpreter's Bible*, vol. 10, 771–1003. Edited by Leander E. Keck. Nashville: Abingdon, 2002.

Shakespeare, William. "Sonnet 73." In *Shakespeare's Sonnets: With Detailed Notes from the World's Leading Center of Shakespeare Studies*, edited by

Barbara A. Mowat and Paul Werstine, 165. New York: Washington Square Press, 2004.

Thulstrup, Marie Mikulová. "Kierkegaard's Dialectic of Imitation." In *A Kierkegaard Critique: An International Selection of Essays Interpreting Kierkegaard*, edited by Howard A. Johnson and Niels Thulstrup, 266–85. New York: Harper, 1962.

Wahl, Jean. "Kierkegaard et le Mysticisme." *Hermès* 1 [1930]: 16-23

Walsh, Sylvia. *Living Poetically: Kierkegaard's Existential Aesthetics.* University Park: Pennsylvania State University Press, 1994.

Watkin, Julia. *Historical Dictionary of Kierkegaard's Philosophy.* Lanham, MD: The Scarecrow Press, Inc., 2001.

Wesley, John. "A Second Letter to the Rev. Dr. Free." In *The Works of John Wesley*, vol. 9, 321–30. Edited by Rupert E. Davies. Nashville: Abingdon, 1989.

———. "A Short History of the People Called Methodists." In *The Works of John Wesley*, vol. 9, 425–503. Edited by Rupert E. Davies. Nashville: Abingdon, 1989.

Wolf, Kenneth Baxter. *The Poverty of Riches: St. Francis of Assisi Reconsidered.* Oxford: Oxford University Press, 2003.

Index of Kierkegaard's Works

Index of Names and Subjects

Barnett, Christopher B.,
*Kierkegaard, Pietism and
Holiness*, xiv
Barrett, Lee C., 31n23, 180n228
Barth, Karl, 18n48
beauty: and aesthetics, 64n4;
Balthasar on loss of, 65–66, 76 ;
channel to holy, 122 ;
contemplating, 73; effect of
SK's literary touch, 57, 122; of
autumn, 97; of dependence on
God, 37–38; of existence, 96,
98, 168, 150–51; of faith, 79,
138; of love, 120; of natural
world, 91, 104–6, 108, 110,
113, 186; of speech, 178; of
spiritual journey, 134–35; of
time, 97
Berlin, 89
Bernard of Clairvaux, 22, 23; "On
Loving God", 19–21
Bible (books): 1 Corinthians, 13,
160 ; 2 Corinthians, 9, 34n31,
155, 156; Acts, 60; Ecclesiastes,
88; Genesis, 22, 59; James, 27,
100, 124; Job, 149–53; John,
131n1, 138–40, 142; Luke,
54n102, 73, 73n33, 135,
170n186, 176, 176n205, 182;
Mark, 170n186, 54n102;
Matthew, 54, 54n102, 101–2,
173n194; Revelation, 26;
Romans, 87, 158, 160n129

Bible, 4, 9, 10; Hebrew Scriptures,
134, 178; icons of faith in,
131–86
Billede (image, picture, reflection),
68, 76, 78, 80, 146, 149,
165–66, 169, 182; in SK's
authorship, 69–75
birds, xiii, 89, 91–92, 100–117
Bloom, Harold, xi–xii
body, 73, 101, 103, 110, 115, 120
Bonhoeffer, Dietrich, 6
Boring, Eugene M., 102
Brazil, 90
Brorson, Hans Adolph, 8
Brunner, Emil, 18n48

calm, 12, 16, 31n20, 109, 117, 120,
128, 180, 185
Calvary, 170
capacious consciousness, xi–xii
Catholic: literature, xiii, 3, 8, 65,
87; mysticism, 5, 6, 31n23, 59;
spirituality, 7
Catholicism, 3n16, 5, 8, 75n40
Ceylon, 92
change, 23, 27–28, 30, 35, 52,
93–98, 125, 145, 154, 158, 166,
177, 182
choice, 41, 92, 137; between art
and religion, 78; of defiance,
151; of faith, 65, 168, 171; of
God, 115–16; of roads, 90; of
self, 35

pain, 22, 35, 44, 97, 98, 99,
148n69, 150, 151, 157, 159,
166, 179, 186
Palestine, 131
pantheism, 118
paradise, 179
paradox, 100; absolute, 45; of
ascent lit., 42; of despair, 49,
54; of faith, 74, 99; of sinner
woman, 163; of spiritual
journey, 31n23, 44, 45, 47; of
worship, 84
passivity, 105, 176
patience, 73, 74, 159
patriarchy, 183
patristic era, 113, 173
Pattison, George, xi, 18, 18n48,
64, 65, 68, 70, 170, 173n195
Paul of Tarsus, xiv, 9, 13, 22,
34n31, 60, 87; icon of faith,
xiv, 135, 148, 154-59, 160, 163
Peter, Apostle, 135
Pharisee(s), 144-46, 176, 179, 180
Pietism, xiii, xiv, 2, 3, 3n16, 4-10,
15, 27n2, 31n23, 37n55, 59,
165
piety, 4, 72, 144, 151, 182-83,
184n244
Plato, 64n4, 99
pleasure, 6, 34, 38, 59, 84, 98, 99,
121, 124-25, 140, 155
Podmore, Simon, 56-57n112, 156
Polk, Timothy Houston, 134

powerlessness, 74, 138,139n30,
157
prayer, 4, 16n46, 31, 37, 132, 133,
137, 144, 161, 165
Protestantism, 3, 6, 59, 87;
literature, xiii, 8, 59; Reformed
thought, 66, 31n23
prototype, 149, 164, 170, 171, 182,
184, 184n244, 186. *See also*
Forbillede
providence, 102, 108, 175
Przywara, Erich, 75n40
pseudonymity, xii, 10-11, 40, 42,
47, 71, 77, 95n30, 100, 120,
136, 137, 139n30, 143, 152,
165
purgatory, 158
purity of heart, 121, 124, 126-28

quietness, state of mind, 123-24

Rae, Murray, 172
reason and faith, 147-48
recollection, religious and
aesthetic, 97-100
reflection: aesthetic, 64, 64n4, 65,
69-70; and autumn, 95;
infinite, 152; of eternal, 74, 75;
on Bible, 10
religion, xiv, 15, 43, 63, 67, 68, 71,
76, 78, 165; of the book, 131
religious, the, 11-13, 23, 40, 42,
44, 61, 65, 67, 68, 71, 72, 136,

understanding, 144; -will,
56n112, 121, 125
Sermon on the Mount, 101, 124
sign: Christ as, 164-65, 167,
169-71, 174; language as, 132;
of contradiction, 167, 174; of
dishonesty, 44; of distinction,
111; of faith, 153; of God, 28
; of inner human, 89; of self-
dispossession, 185; of SK's
influences, 38n59
signed writings, xii, 17, 111, 136,
137, 139n30, 143
silence, 73 104, 117, 123, 124, 132
sin, 59, 146, 176; and despair, 47,
52-54, 98, 99, 128; and faith,
55, 134, 145, 160; and love,
178-81; and mercy, 144, 184
single-mindedness, 5n20, 90, 124,
128, 184
Socrates, 100
Solomon, 101, 105
sorrow, 53, 58, 148, 150, 153, 154,
159, 169, 180, 184
soul, 41, 59, 74, 99, 118, 120, 153,
182
sound: and silence, 132; autumn,
95; mediating Christ, 165;
natural and spiritual, 92, 128
Spener, Philipp Jakob, 4
Spirit: Holy, 54, 163; of love, 161;
transfigured self as, 57n112

spirit: and matter, 103, 115;
finitized, 16n46; human's
glory, 111; *spiritus*, 16
spiritual: burden of earthly life,
112; core of human, 17, 32;
death, 73, 106; demons, 111;
development, 47, 84, 118;
dishonesty, 44; foundation, 14;
fulfillment, 41, 85; growth, 23,
24, 38, 39, 133; healing, 108;
icon, 97, 121, 122; imbalance,
107; imprisonment, 157;
itinerary, xiii, 26, 39, 45;
journey, 16, 25, 31, 31n23, 34,
39, 43-44, 46, 54, 57n112, 63,
93, 133, 135, 136, 142, 148;
joy, 154, 157; ladder, 54   ;
life, 14, 17, 23, 27, 47, 50, 55,
60, 88, 101, 111, 133, 135, 180,
186; poverty, 42; purity, 97,
121; seeing, 178; sounds, 92,
128; torment, 154; tradition, 3,
19, 42, 53, 133; trial, 56n112,
137, 155-57; truth, 176;
wholeness, 182; writers, xiii, 8,
19, 37n55, 59, 60
spirituality: and mysticism, 5n20;
Catholic, 7; Christ-centered, 6,
8, 45, 174; Christian, xiiin5,
xiv, 5n20, 17, 19, 25, 42, 53,
57, 57n112, 59, 84, 134, 136,
173, 183; defined, 16, 16n46,
17; goal of, 17, 39, 43, 53, 60,
84, 180; inwardness, 16n46;

CPSIA information can be obtained at www.ICGtesting.com
Printed in the USA
LVOW12s2154270614

391994LV00005B/6/P